MW01047569

THE WONDERS OF SCIENCE

MATTER, MOTION, AND MACHINES

Joan S. Gottlieb

Steck-Vaughn Company

A Subsidiary of National Education Corporation

ISBN 0-8114-4139-3

5 6 7 8 9 0 DBH 94

TABLE OF CONTENTS

What Is Matter?

Different Types of Matter

What do water, a rock, and a dog have in common? They are all made of **matter.** You are made of matter. Everything you see or touch is matter. The whole world around you is made of matter.

Matter is anything that takes up space and has **mass.** What is mass? Mass is a measure of how much matter an object has. For example, a mountain takes up space and has mass. A rock takes up space and has mass. A mountain has more mass than a rock. But they are both matter. A kitten has less mass than a tiger. But they are both matter.

In everyday life, mass is about the same as weight. But to a scientist, mass is different from weight. The mass of an object never changes. It is always the same. But the weight of an object can change. Weight is the pull that **gravity** has on an object.

Gravity is a force. The gravity of Earth pulls on all matter near Earth. Gravity pulls matter toward the ground. Gravity is why anything you drop falls to the ground. Without gravity, you would float in the air.

Gravity is strongest at the center of Earth. Far from the center, at the top of a mountain, gravity is weaker. Suppose you were in a deep hole in Earth. Gravity would be strong. It would pull hard on you. So you would weigh more than you would weigh on top of a mountain. Farther from Earth's center, gravity does not pull as hard.

A. Answer True or False.

1. You are made of matter. _____

2. A kitten is not made of matter. _____

3. Matter is anything that takes up space and has mass. _____

4. To a scientist, mass is the same as weight. _____

5. Weight is the pull that gravity has on an object. _____

6. Gravity is the strongest at the center of Earth. _____

7. Farther from Earth's center, gravity pulls harder. _____

B. Write the letter for the correct answer.

1. Anything that takes up space and has mass is _____.
   (a) gravity   (b) matter   (c) weight

2. The pull that gravity has on an object is the object's _____.
   (a) space   (b) weight   (c) mass

3. Everything you see or touch is _____.
   (a) gravity   (b) weight   (c) matter

4. Gravity is _____ at the center of Earth.
   (a) strongest   (b) hottest   (c) weakest

5. Matter is pulled to the ground by _____.
   (a) space   (b) air   (c) gravity

C. Remember that gravity is strongest at the center of Earth. For each pair of places, write X where the weight of an object would be greater.

1. down in a deep hole _____

   on top of a mountain _____

2. in an airplane in the air _____

   in an airport on the ground _____

3. in a spaceship about to take off from the launching pad _____

   in a spaceship traveling in outer space _____

Solid

Liquid

Gas

A brick, milk, steam, and lightning are all matter. But they are in different **states.** Matter can exist in four states. Matter can be **solid,** like a brick. It can be **liquid,** like milk. It can be a **gas,** like steam. Or it can be **plasma,** like lightning.

All matter is made up of tiny particles. What state the matter is in depends on the way these particles move and are held together.

In a solid, the particles are held very close together. For this reason, solids have a certain shape. A brick stays the same shape. You can break a brick, but you cannot mold it into another shape.

In a liquid, the particles are not held together as tightly as in a solid. Because the particles in a liquid are farther apart, liquid matter does not have its own shape. Liquid matter takes the shape of the container you put it in. When milk is in a carton, it is shaped like the carton. If you pour milk into a glass, it takes the shape of the glass. The particles in a liquid can move around easily and quickly to fit any container.

In a gas, the particles are far apart from one another. They move around quickly in their container. The steam coming out of a tea kettle mixes with the air and spreads out into the room.

Most of the matter in the universe is plasma. The sun and most of the stars you see in the sky are plasma. But plasma is a state of matter that is not common on Earth. Lightning is a kind of plasma.

A. Write the letter for the correct answer.

1. Most of the matter in the universe is _____.
   (a) plasma   (b) liquid   (c) gas

2. The particles in a liquid _____.
   (a) are held very close together   (b) can move around
   (c) cannot move

3. Steam is a _____.
   (a) solid   (b) liquid   (c) gas

4. A brick is _____.
   (a) plasma   (b) solid   (c) liquid

5. In a solid, the particles are very _____.
   (a) close together   (b) far apart   (c) fast moving

6. In a gas, the particles are very _____.
   (a) close together   (b) slow moving   (c) far apart

B. Answer True or False.

1. Solid, liquid, gas, and plasma are the states of matter. _____

2. Matter can be solid like a brick. _____

3. In a gas, the particles are far apart from one another. _____

4. The sun is plasma. _____

5. In a solid, the particles are far apart from one another. _____

6. The particles in a liquid cannot move around. _____

7. Solids do not have any certain shape. _____

C. List the four states of matter. Write an example of each state.

1. _____   example: _____

2. _____   example: _____

3. _____   example: _____

4. _____   example: _____

Atoms

8 Neutrons

8 Protons

8 Electrons

An oxygen atom has 8 positive protons and 8 neutrons in its nucleus, and 8 negative electrons speeding around the nucleus.

Everything is made of **atoms.** Atoms are tiny pieces of matter. They are too small to see even under a microscope. In fact, the smallest piece of matter you can see under a microscope has 10 billion atoms.

Atoms are made of even tinier bits of matter. There are three kinds of particles in atoms. They are **protons, neutrons,** and **electrons.** All electrons are exactly the same. All protons are alike, too. So are all neutrons. If all atoms are made of the same kinds of particles, how are atoms different?

Different kinds of atoms are different from each other because they contain a different number of particles. A carbon atom has six protons, six neutrons, and six electrons. Oxygen has eight protons, eight neutrons, and eight electrons. Oxygen is different from carbon because it has more particles. Each kind of atom has a different number of the three particles.

Protons and neutrons are in the center, or **nucleus,** of the atom. Electrons are much smaller than protons and neutrons. Electrons move around the nucleus at great speeds. Because electrons move so fast, it is impossible to tell exactly where an electron is at any one time.

The particles that are in atoms have different **electric charges.** Electrons have a negative electric charge. Protons have a positive electric charge. Neutrons have no electric charge. An atom with the same number of electrons and protons also has no electric charge. An atom without an electric charge is called a neutral atom.

A. Draw lines to complete the sentences.

1. Atoms   have a positive electric charge.

2. Electrons   are made of protons, neutrons, and electrons.

3. Neutrons   have a negative electric charge.

4. Protons   have no electric charge.

5. The nucleus   is made of protons and neutrons.

B. Write the letter for the correct answer.

1. Atoms are made of three small _____.
   (a) elements   (b) particles   (c) electrons

2. All electrons are _____.
   (a) exactly the same   (b) positive   (c) different

3. Different kinds of atoms are different from each other because they contain a different _____ of particles.
   (a) size   (b) number   (c) speed

4. Protons and neutrons are in the center, or _____, of the atom.
   (a) nucleus   (b) electron   (c) charge

5. Protons have _____.
   (a) negative charges   (b) positive charges   (c) no charge

6. Because electrons _____, it is impossible to tell exactly where an electron is at any one time.
   (a) move too slowly   (b) do not move   (c) move so fast

7. Neutrons have _____.
   (a) positive charges   (b) negative charges
   (c) no electric charge

C. Use each word to write a sentence about the parts of an atom.

1. proton _____

_____

2. electron _____

_____

Elements

The iron in the gate, the gold in the jewelry, and the hydrogen and oxygen in the water are all elements.

Elements are the simplest form of matter. An element is matter that is made of only one kind of atom. All the atoms of an element are exactly the same. Gold is an element. All the atoms in a bar of gold are the same. Oxygen is also an element. Every oxygen atom is exactly the same. But oxygen atoms are very different from gold atoms.

Because elements are made of only one kind of atom, they cannot be broken down into different substances. No matter how tiny you cut an element, it will still be the element. One atom of gold is still gold.

You can think of an element as being like sand. Grains of sand are like the atoms in an element. The grains are all alike. You can separate sand any way you like, but it is still sand. Even a single grain of sand is still sand.

Every element is different from all other elements. Atoms of one element have a different number of particles than atoms of every other element. Only oxygen atoms have eight of each particle. Every other element has a different number.

Most elements are found in nature. Iron is an element that is found inside Earth. Wrought iron gates, fireplace grates, and bathtubs are made of iron. Gold is also an element that is found on Earth. Jewelry is often made of gold.

Some matter is made of more than one element. The air you breathe is oxygen, nitrogen, and other elements. Water is made of the elements hydrogen and oxygen. All matter is made of elements.

A. Fill in the missing words.

1. Elements are the simplest form of _____ . (iron, matter)

2. An element is matter that is made of only one kind of _____.
   (atom, sand)

3. Every element is _____ all other elements.
   (different from, the same as)

4. Elements _____ be broken down into different substances.
   (can, cannot)

5. Fireplace grates and bathtubs are made of the element _____.
   (gold, iron)

6. The air you breathe is _____ element.
   (one, more than one)

7. All matter is made of _____. (elements, sand)

8. Atoms of one element have a different _____ of particles
   than atoms of every other element. (kind, number)

B. Make a list of at least three elements.

_____

_____

_____

C. Answer True or False.

1. Elements are the simplest form of matter. _____

2. An element is made of many different kinds of atoms. _____

3. Every element is the same as every other element. _____

4. Elements can be broken down into other substances. _____

5. Iron and gold are elements. _____

6. Oxygen is one of the elements in air. _____

7. Some matter is made of more than one element. _____

8. Water is made of the elements iron and gold. _____

Things made of metal are everywhere.

There are 109 elements. Most of the elements are **metals.** You see metals around you every day. Gold and silver are metals. So is iron.

All metals have some things in common. They are all shiny. Light bounces off metal surfaces and makes them gleam. For this reason, metals are often used for decoration.

Metals **conduct** heat. Heat passes easily through metal and into other objects. That is why pots for cooking are made of metals.

Metals also conduct electricity. Electricity passes through metal easily. In addition, metals are **ductile,** or easily shaped into a new form. This means that they can be pulled into a thin wire. Because metals are ductile and conduct electricity, wire made of metals such as copper is used to carry electricity.

Many metals are easy to shape. They can be made into jewelry. Aluminum can be made into thin sheets of aluminum foil. Gold can be made into thin sheets of gold leaf. The torch of the Statue of Liberty is covered with gold leaf.

There are even metals in your body. Calcium and magnesium are metals that help make your bones. Sodium is a metal that your body needs to work properly. There is sodium in table salt.

People have found thousands of uses for metals. We buy things with coins made of metal. We travel in cars, trains, and planes made of metal. We use tools and machines made of metal. Metals are part of our daily lives.

A. Fill in the missing words.

1. Most of the elements are _____. (metals, iron)

2. Metals are _____. (shiny, black)

3. Metals _____ heat and electricity. (stop, conduct)

4. Metals can be pulled _____.
   (apart, into thin wire)

5. Gold and aluminum can be made into _____.
   (sodium, thin sheets)

6. Calcium and magnesium are metals that help make your _____.
   (hair, bones)

7. People have found thousands of uses for _____.
   (sodium, metals)

B. Answer True or False.

1. There is sodium in table salt. _____

2. Metals are not shiny. _____

3. Metals conduct heat and electricity. _____

4. Metals cannot be pulled into thin wire. _____

5. Gold can be made into thin sheets called gold leaf. _____

6. Your body does not have metals in it. _____

C. Write M after statements that describe metals.

1. They are black. _____

2. Electricity will not pass through them. _____

3. They are shiny. _____

4. They can be pulled into a thin wire. _____

5. They let heat pass through them. _____

6. People have not found many uses for them. _____

The metalloid silicon is part of the substance that makes up sand.

Silicon is used to make the tiny chips that make computers run.

A small number of the elements are not metals. These elements are divided into three types: **metalloids, nonmetals,** and **inert gases.**

Metalloids are elements that are like metals in some ways. They are shiny like metals. But they do not conduct heat and electricity as well as metals do. Silicon is a metalloid. Sand is made mostly of silicon. There is silicon in glass. The chips that make computers work are also made of silicon.

Nonmetals are not like metals at all. They are not shiny. They do not conduct heat or electricity well. They cannot be used to make wire. Nonmetals can be solids, liquids, or gases. Carbon is a solid nonmetal. Diamonds are made of carbon that has been squeezed together underground. Carbon is one of the elements that forms your body. Bromine is a liquid nonmetal. Small amounts of bromine are in seawater. Oxygen and nitrogen are nonmetals that are gases. The air you breathe is made up mostly of oxygen and nitrogen.

The inert gases are a special group of gases. Helium is an inert gas. A balloon filled with helium will float in the air because helium is lighter than air.

A. Fill in the missing words.

1. A _____ number of the elements are not metals. (small, large)

2. Silicon is a _____. (gas, metalloid)

3. Nonmetals are not like _____ at all. (metals, liquids)

4. Diamonds are made of _____. (sand, carbon)

5. Bromine is a _____ nonmetal. (liquid, solid)

6. Oxygen and nitrogen are two nonmetals that are _____. (shiny, gases)

7. Helium is _____. (an inert gas, a metal)

B. Answer True or False.

1. All elements are metals. _____

2. Metalloids are shiny. _____

3. Metalloids conduct heat and electricity just as well as metals do. _____

4. Nonmetals can be solids, liquids, or gases. _____

5. Carbon is a nonmetal. _____

6. Air is made up mostly of oxygen and nitrogen. _____

7. A balloon filled with oxygen will float in the air because oxygen is lighter than air. _____

8. The inert gases are a special group of metalloids. _____

C. Draw lines to complete the sentences.

1. Helium   is a nonmetal that is a gas.

2. Oxygen   is an inert gas.

3. Bromine   is a liquid nonmetal.

4. Nonmetals   are not like metals at all.

5. Metalloids   are like metals in some ways.

Periodic Table

Part of the Periodic Table, Through Atomic Number 54

I	II												III	IV	V	VI	VII	VIII
1 H Hydrogen																		2 He Helium
3 Li Lithium	4 Be Beryllium												5 B Boron	6 C Carbon	7 N Nitrogen	8 O Oxygen	9 F Fluorine	10 Ne Neon
11 Na Sodium	12 Mg Magnesium												13 Al Aluminum	14 Si Silicon	15 P Phosphorus	16 S Sulfur	17 Cl Chlorine	18 Ar Argon
19 K Potassium	20 Ca Calcium	21 SC Scandium	22 Ti Titanium	23 V Vanadium	24 Cr Chromium	25 Mn Manganese	26 Fe Iron	27 Co Cobalt	28 Ni Nickel	29 Cu Copper	30 Zn Zinc		31 Ga Gallium	32 Ge Germanium	33 As Arsenic	34 Se Selenium	35 Br Bromine	36 Kr Krypton
37 Rb Rubidium	38 Sr Strontium	39 Y Yttrium	40 Zr Zirconium	41 Nb Niobium	42 Mo Molybdenum	43 Tc Technetium	44 Ru Ruthenium	45 Rh Rhodium	46 Pd Palladium	47 Ag Silver	48 Cd Cadmium		49 In Indium	50 Sn Tin	51 Sb Antimony	52 Te Tellurium	53 I Iodine	54 Xe Xenon

atomic number — 12

symbol of element — Mg

element name — Magnesium

Elements above and to the right of this line are nonmetals.

Elements below and to the left of this line are metals.

Scientists have organized all the elements in a chart called the **periodic table.** It lists the 109 elements in rows and columns. Elements similar to one another are in the same column. Scientists can tell a lot about an element from where it is found in the periodic table.

The elements are arranged in rows according to their **atomic numbers.** The atomic number of an element is the number of protons in the nucleus of one of its atoms. Oxygen has eight protons. The atomic number of oxygen is 8. No two elements have the same atomic number.

All elements in the periodic table have symbols. O is the symbol for oxygen. Na is the symbol for sodium. Scientists use these symbols in formulas. The formula for water is H_2O. The "H" stands for hydrogen. The "$_2$" means there are two hydrogen atoms for every oxygen atom.

Fill in the missing words.

1. No two elements have the same _____ number. (periodic, atomic)

2. Every element has a _____. (symbol, formula)

3. O is the symbol for _____. (water, oxygen)

Review

Part A

Fill in the missing words.

1. Everything you see or touch is _____. (gas, matter)

2. Matter is anything that takes up space and has _____. (oxygen, mass)

3. Matter can exist in four _____. (states, places)

4. Everything is made of _____. (carbon, atoms)

5. Atoms are different because they contain different _____ of particles. (numbers, colors)

6. Electrons are much _____ than protons and neutrons. (larger, smaller)

7. The simplest form of matter is _____. (an element, liquid)

8. Elements cannot be _____ other substances. (broken down into, mixed with)

9. Heat and electricity pass through _____ easily. (inert gases, metals)

10. Elements are organized in the _____ table. (periodic, atomic)

Part B

Read each sentence. Write True if the sentence is True. Write False if the sentence is false.

1. Gravity makes anything you drop float in the air. _____

2. Weight is the pull that gravity has on an object. _____

3. Liquid matter takes the shape of the container you put it in. _____

4. Atoms are made up of electrons, protons, and neutrons. _____

5. Every electron is different from every other electron. _____

6. Elements are made up of many different kinds of atoms. _____

7. Nonmetals can be solids, liquids, or gases. _____

Fill in the circle in front of the word or phrase that best completes the sentences. The first one is done for you.

1. Anything that takes up space and has mass is
   - ⓐ a solid.
   - ● matter.
   - ⓒ an element.

2. How much matter an object has is its
   - ⓐ mass.
   - ⓑ atomic number.
   - ⓒ gravity.

3. The mass of an object
   - ⓐ sometimes changes.
   - ⓑ always changes.
   - ⓒ never changes.

4. Lightning is a kind of
   - ⓐ solid.
   - ⓑ liquid.
   - ⓒ plasma.

5. Atoms are very
   - ⓐ heavy.
   - ⓑ tiny.
   - ⓒ large.

6. The particles in atoms have different
   - ⓐ electric charges.
   - ⓑ gases.
   - ⓒ flavors.

7. Most elements are found in
   - ⓐ the kitchen.
   - ⓑ space.
   - ⓒ nature.

8. Most of the elements are
   - ⓐ nonmetals.
   - ⓑ metals.
   - ⓒ inert gases.

9. Elements are arranged in the periodic table according to their
   - ⓐ atomic number.
   - ⓑ color.
   - ⓒ weight.

10. The formula for water is
   - ⓐ H_2O.
   - ⓑ O.
   - ⓒ Na.

Just for Fun

Fill in the missing words in each sentence. Use the words below.

atomic	gravity	mass	table
charges	leaf	metals	weight
element	liquid	solid	

1. Elements that are shiny and conduct heat are __ __ __ __ __ __.
   14   7

2. How much matter an object has is its __ __ __ __.
   10

3. The number of protons in the nucleus of an atom of an element is its
   __ __ __ __ __ __ number.
   18   5 17

4. The force that pulls matter toward the ground is __ __ __ __ __ __ __.
   6   20

5. The simplest form of matter is an __ __ __ __ __ __ __.
   21   11

6. The pull of gravity on an object is the object's __ __ __ __ __ __.
   4   19

7. Elements are organized in a periodic __ __ __ __ __.
   1 12   3

8. Electrons have negative __ __ __ __ __ __ __.
   2   22

9. A brick is a __ __ __ __ __.
   15   8

10. The metal gold can be made into sheets of gold __ __ __ __.
    16

11. Milk is a __ __ __ __ __ __.
    9   13

Solve the Secret Message. When a letter of a word above has a number
under it, write that letter above the same number in the Secret Message.

Secret Message:

__ __ __   __ __ __ __ __   __ __   __ __ __ __   __ __   __ __ __ __ __ __.
1 2 3   4 5 6 7 8   9 10   11 12 13 14   15 16   17 18 19 20 21 22

UNIT 2 · Changes in Matter
Molecules and Compounds

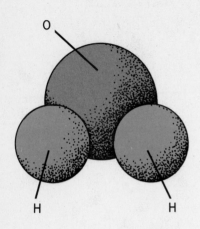

Water Molecule, H_2O

A **molecule** is a group of atoms. Most matter can be broken down into molecules. Elements are made of only one kind of atom. So the molecules of an element contain only one kind of atom.

A **compound** is a substance that is made from molecules of more than one element. Water is a compound. In Unit 1, you learned that the formula for water is H_2O. This formula means that there are two atoms of hydrogen and one atom of oxygen in each water molecule.

Atoms of different elements join together to form molecules of a compound. A new substance is formed. This substance differs from the elements it is made of.

An atom is the smallest bit of an element that is still that element. In the same way, a molecule is the smallest bit of a compound that is still that compound. A water molecule has two atoms of hydrogen and one atom of oxygen. But these atoms are not water until they combine to form a molecule.

Every molecule in a compound is exactly the same. The formula for a compound is like a recipe for one molecule of the compound. If you follow the recipe, you always come out with the same compound. Compounds form in different ways. Have you ever seen iron rust? It turns red-brown and forms flakes. Rust is a compound. When iron gets wet, it can combine with oxygen from the air to form the compound rust. The symbol for iron is Fe. The formula for rust is Fe_2O_3.

A. Fill in the missing words.

1. A molecule is a group of _____. (atoms, formulas)

2. Most matter can be broken down into _____. (compounds, molecules)

3. A compound is made from molecules of _____ element. (one, more than one)

4. Water is a _____. (solid, compound)

5. A _____ is the smallest bit of a compound that is still that compound. (molecule, substance)

6. Every molecule in a compound is _____. (different, exactly the same)

7. When iron gets wet, it can combine with oxygen from the air to form the compound _____. (rust, water)

B. Answer True or False.

1. Most matter can be broken down into molecules. _____

2. The formula for water is OH. _____

3. When atoms of different elements form molecules of a compound, a new substance is formed. _____

4. A molecule is the smallest bit of an element that is still that element. _____

5. Rust is a compound. _____

6. The formula for iron is Fe_2O_3. _____

C. Draw lines to complete the sentences.

1. Compounds   is a group of atoms.

2. Water   are made of only one kind of atom.

3. Elements   is a compound.

4. A molecule   form in different ways.

Mixtures

Tuna salad is an example of a mixture.

Lemonade is an example of a solution.

Most of the things you see in everyday life are not pure elements or compounds. They are **mixtures** of different elements and compounds. Some mixtures happen in nature. People also mix elements and compounds to make many different things.

When elements and compounds combine together to form a mixture, no new substances are made. This is because no new molecules are formed. The molecules of the elements and compounds are just mixed together. Scientists can always separate a mixture back into the substances from which it was made.

Mixtures are not always the same. Air is a mixture. Air is different in different places. Air in cities or near factories is dirtier than air in the country. The air in a pine forest smells like pine trees. Air in different places has different molecules in it.

Sometimes you can tell that a substance is a mixture. For example, tuna salad is usually made of tuna, celery, and mayonnaise. You can still see the pieces of tuna and celery in the mixture. You can separate the tuna and the celery out of the tuna salad.

But what about lemonade? It is made of lemon juice and water and sugar, but it does not look like a mixture. It is not easy to separate back into its parts. This kind of mixture is called a **solution.** Most solutions are liquids, but some are solid. If you melted gold and silver and mixed them together and let the mixture harden, it would be a solid solution.

A. Use the words below to complete the sentences.

compound	molecules	separate
mixture	same	solid

1. When elements and compounds combine to form a

    _____, no new substances are made.

2. Scientists can always _____ a mixture back into the
    substances from which it was made.

3. Mixtures are not always the _____.

4. Air in different places has different _____ in it.

5. Most solutions are liquids, but some are _____.

B. Write the letter for the correct answer.

1. Most of the things you see in everyday life are _____.
    (a) metals   (b) mixtures   (c) wood

2. When elements and compounds combine to form a mixture, no new

    _____ are made.
    (a) atoms   (b) liquids   (c) substances

3. Lemonade is an example of a _____.
    (a) molecule   (b) solution   (c) compound

4. Most solutions are _____.
    (a) liquids   (b) gases   (c) elements

C. Answer the questions.

1. Why are no new substances made when elements and compounds

    combine to form a mixture? _____

    _____

2. If you melted gold and silver and mixed them together and then

    let the mixture harden, what would it be? _____

    _____

23

Physical Changes

Water boiling is a physical change.

Wood being sawed is also a physical change.

A **physical change** is any change in matter that does not change the matter's molecules. When any kind of mixture is formed, a physical change takes place. But the molecules that make the mixture do not change.

Another kind of physical change takes place when matter changes states. You know that three of the states of matter are solid, liquid, and gas. A solid or a gas can become a liquid. A liquid can become a solid or a gas. The state that matter is in depends on how close together the molecules are. When matter changes states, the molecules themselves do not change. They just get closer together or farther apart.

At room temperature, water is a liquid. When you boil it, heat makes the molecules in the water move farther apart. The water evaporates, or turns from a liquid into a gas, called steam. If you hold a cold metal spoon in the steam, the steam condenses on the spoon. As heat from the steam passes to the spoon, the steam molecules move closer together, and the gas becomes a liquid again. If you freeze water, the molecules get closer together. It becomes solid ice. When ice is heated, it turns back into a liquid.

A third kind of physical change takes place when there is a change in the shape of the substance. When you saw wood, some of it is changed into sawdust. The molecules in sawdust are the same as the molecules in the piece of wood. Only the shape of the wood has changed.

A. Underline the correct words.

1. A physical change is any change in matter that does not change the matter's (molecules, shape).

2. A physical change takes place when matter changes (color, states).

3. The state that matter is in depends on how close together its (gases, molecules) are.

4. When you boil water, it becomes (steam, ice).

5. Ice is a (gas, solid).

6. When you saw wood, you cause a (chemical, physical) change.

B. Answer <u>True</u> or <u>False</u>.

1. When mixtures are formed, a physical change takes place.

   _____

2. A liquid cannot become a solid or a gas. _____

3. At room temperature, water is a gas. _____

4. If you freeze water, the molecules get closer together, and the water becomes ice. _____

5. A physical change takes place when you change the shape of a substance. _____

6. The molecules in sawdust are different from the molecules in pieces of wood. _____

C. Use each word to write a sentence about the physical changes in matter.

1. water _____

   _____

2. wood _____

   _____

Chemical Changes

Burning wood is a chemical change.

Rusting iron is a chemical change.

A **chemical change** happens whenever there is a change in a substance's molecules. Chemical changes always make new substances. In a chemical change, energy causes the atoms to break free of their molecules and form different molecules.

Burning wood is a chemical change. Wood is changed into new substances—ashes and smoke. The energy of the fire causes the atoms in the wood molecules to break apart. The atoms then form into molecules of ash and smoke. Rusting iron is another chemical change. Iron atoms join with oxygen atoms to form molecules of a new substance. This new substance is rust.

Matter is never lost in a chemical change. There are always exactly the same number of atoms before the chemical change as there are afterward.

Baking causes chemical changes. A cake is made of flour, sugar, milk, and eggs. But eating these things without mixing and baking them is not the same as eating cake! When you bake the mixture, a chemical change takes place. The atoms of the mixture re-form to create atoms of a new substance, cake.

Chemical changes even take place inside your body. In fact, you could not live without them. Chemical changes turn the food you eat into substances your body can use.

A. Fill in the missing words.

1. A chemical change happens whenever there is a change in a substance's _____. (molecules, shape)

2. Chemical changes always make new _____. (atoms, substances)

3. Burning wood is a _____ change. (physical, chemical)

4. When iron atoms join with oxygen atoms, they form _____. (rust, flames)

5. _____ is never lost in a chemical change. (Rust, Matter)

B. Write the letter for the correct answer.

1. A _____ change happens whenever there is a change in a substance's molecules.
   (a) physical   (b) temperature   (c) chemical

2. In a chemical change, _____ causes the atoms to break free of their molecues and form different molecules.
   (a) energy   (b) water   (c) smoke

3. When wood burns, it is changed into ashes and _____.
   (a) water   (b) smoke   (c) oxygen

4. There are always exactly the same number of _____ before a chemical change as there are afterward.
   (a) formulas   (b) compounds   (c) atoms

C. Answer the questions.

1. Why is rusting iron a chemical change? _____

   _____

   _____

2. How do the chemical changes that take place inside your body help you?

   _____

   _____

   _____

Chemical Reactions

+

Oxygen Molecule

Hydrogen Molecules

Water Molecules

Chemical changes are called **chemical reactions.** Scientists have a special way of showing what happens in a chemical reaction. You have learned that every element has a symbol, such as O for oxygen and H for hydrogen. You also know that scientists use these symbols in formulas that describe molecules. H_2O is the formula that describes a water molecule.

In chemical reactions, molecules are changed. Scientists use formulas in equations to show these changes. Instead of an equal sign, chemical equations use an arrow. Because matter is never lost in a chemical reaction, the number of atoms is the same on both sides of the arrow.

This equation shows how hydrogen and oxygen combine to form water.

$$2H_2 + O_2 \rightarrow 2H_2O$$

A drawing of this equation is at the top of the page. On the left side of the equation are two molecules of hydrogen and one molecule of oxygen. Energy causes these molecules to break apart. Then the atoms form new molecules. You can see the new molecules on the right side of the equation. The new molecules are water molecules. You can see that there is the same number of each kind of atom on each side of the equation. No matter has been lost.

A. Write the letter for the correct answer.

1. H is the symbol for _____ .
   (a) hydrogen   (b) oxygen   (c) an atom

2. O is the symbol for _____ .
   (a) oxygen   (b) hydrogen   (c) an atom

3. Formulas describe _____ .
   (a) atoms   (b) molecules   (c) chemical reactions

4. Scientists use formulas in _____ to show chemical changes.
   (a) charts   (b) test tubes   (c) equations

5. Instead of an equal sign, chemical equations use _____ .
   (a) a circle   (b) an arrow   (c) a square

B. Underline the correct words.

1. Chemical changes are called chemical (reactions, events).

2. Every element has a (color, symbol).

3. H_2O is the formula for (water, wood).

4. In a chemical equation, the number of (substances, atoms) is the same on both sides of the arrow.

5. (Energy, Water) causes molecules to break apart.

6. Formulas describe (equations, molecules).

C. Answer the questions.

1. In a chemical equation, why is the number of atoms the same on both sides of the arrow? _____

   _____

   _____

2. What kind of molecule does the formula H_2O describe? _____

   _____

   _____

Acids, Bases, and Salts

Citrus fruits have citric acid in them.

Many detergents have bases in them.

Table salt is one kind of neutral salt.

Most compounds are **acids, bases,** or **salts.** Acids are the chemical opposite of bases. Acids are compounds made of molecules that have a positive electric charge. Bases are compounds made of molecules that have a negative electric charge. For this reason, acids and bases behave together in a special way.

Litmus paper is a special kind of paper. Scientists use litmus paper to tell whether something is an acid or a base. Acids turn blue litmus paper red. Bases turn red litmus paper blue.

Acids taste sour. Some of them can burn your skin. Some are weak. Weak acids are found in many kinds of food. Other acids are strong. Some strong acids can dissolve metal! Bases taste bitter. They feel soapy and slippery. Some bases can burn your skin. Bases that can be dissolved in water are called **alkalis.**

Acids and alkalis neutralize each other. This means that the negative electric charge of the alkali balances the positive electric charge of the acid. When a certain amount of acid and alkali is mixed together, a chemical change takes place. The acid and alkali turn into a neutral salt and water. Neutral salts cannot burn the skin like acids and bases. Table salt is one kind of neutral salt.

Acids and bases have many uses. Acids in your stomach help you digest food. Acids are used in making many things, such as paper. Bases are often used in cleansers. Both acids and bases are used in making some kinds of cloth.

A. Use the words below to complete the sentences.

alkalis	neutral	positive
bases	neutralize	salts

1. Most compounds are acids, bases, or _____ .

2. Acids are the chemical opposite of _____ .

3. Acids are compounds made of molecules that have a _____ electric charge.

4. Bases that can be dissolved in water are called _____ .

5. Acids and alkalis _____ each other.

6. Table salt is one kind of _____ salt.

B. Answer True or False.

1. Acids taste sour. _____

2. Acids cannot burn your skin. _____

3. Weak acids are found in many kinds of food. _____

4. Bases taste sweet. _____

5. The molecules of bases do not have an electric charge. _____

6. Acids and alkalis neutralize each other. _____

7. There are acids in your stomach that help you digest food.

   _____

8. Bases are often used in cleansers. _____

C. Draw lines to complete the sentences.

1. Bases   turn blue litmus paper red.

2. Acids   feel soapy and slippery.

3. Alkalis   cannot burn your skin.

4. Salts   are bases that can be dissolved in water.

Chemicals Are Everywhere!

All these things have chemicals in them.

Chemicals are an important part of the world around you. You use hundreds of chemicals every day. They can help you to stay healthy.

There are chemicals in the food you eat. Protein is a chemical found in meat, fish, cheese, eggs, and beans. Protein helps you grow and build a strong body. Carbohydrates, the chemicals found in bread, cereal, pasta, and vegetables, give you energy. Vitamins and minerals are chemicals that help your body to use food. Sometimes chemicals are added to food to keep it fresh or give it a different taste.

Chemicals help you keep clean and healthy. They help you clean your home, too. Soap, shampoo, toothpaste, and detergents are all made of chemicals. Medicine is made of chemicals, too. The chemicals in medicine help your body fight disease.

Answer True or False.

1. There are not any chemicals in the food you eat. _____

2. Protein is a chemical found in meat, fish, cheese, eggs, and beans. _____

3. Carbohydrates are chemicals that give you energy. _____

4. Medicine is not made of chemicals. _____

■ Review

Part A

Use the words below to complete the sentences.

chemical	mixtures	physical
compound	molecule	reactions
condenses	neutralize	solution

1. A _____ is a group of atoms.

2. A _____ is a substance that is made from molecules of more than one element.

3. Most of the things you see in everyday life are _____.

4. A mixture that does not look like a mixture and is not easy to separate back into its parts is called a _____.

5. A _____ change is any change in matter that does not change the matter's molecules.

6. If you hold a cold metal spoon in steam, the steam _____ on the spoon.

7. A _____ change happens whenever there is a change in a substance's molecules.

8. Chemical changes are called chemical _____.

9. Acids and alkalis _____ each other.

Part B

Read each sentence. Write <u>True</u> if the sentence is true. Write <u>False</u> if the sentence is false.

1. Every molecule in a compound is exactly the same. _____

2. Chemical changes always make new substances. _____

3. Acids taste bitter and feel soapy and slippery. _____

4. There are chemicals in the food you eat. _____

■ UNIT 2 ▪ Test ■

Fill in the circle in front of the word or phrase that best completes the sentences. The first one is done for you.

1. A molecule is a group of
   - ● atoms.
   - ⓑ elements.
   - ⓒ mixtures.

2. Every molecule in a compound is
   - ⓐ different.
   - ⓑ soft.
   - ⓒ exactly the same.

3. Scientists can always separate a mixture back into
   - ⓐ water and salt.
   - ⓑ the substances from which it was made.
   - ⓒ hydrogen and oxygen.

4. A physical change is any change in matter that does not change the matter's
   - ⓐ state.
   - ⓑ shape.
   - ⓒ molecules.

5. If you heat ice, it turns back into a
   - ⓐ liquid.
   - ⓑ gas.
   - ⓒ solid.

6. Chemical changes always make
   - ⓐ water.
   - ⓑ new substances.
   - ⓒ acids.

7. A chemical change happens when there is a change in a substance's
   - ⓐ state.
   - ⓑ shape.
   - ⓒ molecules.

8. Acids are the chemical opposite of
   - ⓐ metals.
   - ⓑ bases.
   - ⓒ water.

9. Bases that can be dissolved in water are called
   - ⓐ alkalis.
   - ⓑ acids.
   - ⓒ metalloids.

10. The chemical protein is found in
    - ⓐ bread.
    - ⓑ pasta.
    - ⓒ meat.

Just for Fun

Use the clues to complete the puzzle. Choose from the words below.

acids	chemical	liquid	salt
ashes	energy	medicine	solution
bases	freeze	rust	water

Across

3. When wood burns, it turns into smoke and this.
6. Lemonade is an example of this kind of mixture.
8. H_2O is the formula for this.
10. This helps your body fight disease.
11. Water is in this state when it is at room temperature.

Down

1. These are compounds that feel soapy and slippery and have molecules with a negative electric charge.
2. Baking causes this kind of change.
4. Iron atoms join with oxygen atoms to form molecules of this new substance.
5. In a chemical change, this causes the atoms to break free of their molecules and form different molecules.
7. If you do this to water, it changes from a liquid to a solid.
9. These are compounds that taste sour and have molecules with a positive electric charge.

UNIT 3 • Nature's Energies
What Is Energy?

You use energy to play volleyball, and a car uses energy to move.

Imagine you have been swimming for a long time. You are tired. Some friends ask you to play volleyball. You say that you do not have the energy. What exactly do you mean? What is energy?

Energy is the ability to do work. Moving things is a type of work. When you hit a volleyball, you move it. When you jump and run, you move yourself. Playing volleyball, jumping, and running all take energy.

There are several kinds of energy. One kind of energy is **mechanical energy.** Whenever anything moves, it is using mechanical energy. A second kind of energy is **heat energy.** Heat energy passes heat from one object to another. A third kind of energy is **electric energy.** Electric energy makes light bulbs light up and radios play. A fourth kind of energy is **chemical energy.** Gasoline has chemical energy. When gasoline is burned in a car's engine, the chemical energy is changed to mechanical energy. The mechanical energy moves the car.

Energy is not matter, because it does not have mass or take up space. You cannot see energy, but you can see what energy does. Each kind of energy can change into other kinds of energy. In this unit you will learn about different kinds of energy.

A. Use the words below to complete the sentences.

chemical	Energy	matter
Electric	Heat	mechanical

1. _____ is the ability to do work.

2. Whenever anything moves, it is using _____ energy.

3. _____ energy passes heat from one object to another.

4. _____ energy makes light bulbs light up and radios play.

5. Gasoline has _____ energy.

6. Energy is not _____ .

B. Answer <u>True</u> or <u>False</u>.

1. There is only one kind of energy. _____

2. When you jump and run, you do work. _____

3. Gasoline has heat energy. _____

4. Each kind of energy can change into other kinds of energy.

   _____

5. It does not take energy to hit a volleyball. _____

6. Heat energy passes heat from one object to another. _____

7. Energy has mass and takes up space. _____

C. Answer the questions.

1. What are four kinds of energy? _____

   _____

   _____

2. What is energy? _____

   _____

Energy From the Sun

Carbon Dioxide From the Air

Water From the Soil

Plants need the energy of the sun to make food from water and carbon dioxide.

All the energy in the world comes from the sun. The sun's energy is called **solar energy.** On Earth, solar energy is changed to other kinds of energy. Nothing on Earth could live without energy from the sun.

Plants could not live without solar energy. Plants make their own food. They use energy from the sun to make their food. They make food out of water from the soil and the gas in air called carbon dioxide. People eat the food that plants make. Apples, potatoes, lettuce, celery, and beans are all plant foods that people eat. Without solar energy, people would not have any plants to eat.

Some animals also eat plants. Animals eat other animals that eat plants. Without plants, animals could not live. There would be no animals for people to eat. You would not have chicken or hamburgers or fish to eat. You would not have the things that animals produce, such as milk, eggs, or wool, either.

People are warmed by the heat of the sun. When it is cold, people use fuels such as coal and oil to heat their homes. These fuels were made by solar energy. Coal and oil were formed from plants and animals that lived millions of years ago. When the plants and animals died, their bodies became part of Earth. The energy from these dead plants and animals became the chemical energy in coal and oil. When coal and oil are burned, the stored chemical energy becomes heat energy.

A. Write the letter for the correct answer.

1. All energy comes from _____.
   (a) plants   (b) animals   (c) the sun

2. Plants could not live without _____ energy.
   (a) fuel   (b) solar   (c) mechanical

3. Plants make their own _____.
   (a) energy   (b) food   (c) water

4. The energy from dead plants and animals became the _____ energy in coal and oil.
   (a) chemical   (b) mechanical   (c) electric

5. When fuels are burned, chemical energy becomes _____ energy.
   (a) mechanical   (b) electric   (c) heat

B. Name the three things that plants use to make their own food. Choose from the words below.

| carbon dioxide | energy from the sun |
| coal | water from the soil |

1. _____

2. _____

3. _____

C. Answer True or False.

1. All energy comes from the sun. _____

2. Without solar energy, people would not have any plants to eat.

   _____

3. Energy from the sun is called food energy. _____

4. On Earth, solar energy is changed into other kinds of energy.

   _____

5. Coal and oil were formed from carbon dioxide and water. _____

39

Heat Energy

Hot soup heats a metal spoon by conduction.

Convection currents heat water.

The sun heats by radiation.

Heat energy is energy passed as heat from one object to another. Heat always passes from a hotter object to a cooler object. If you hold an ice cube in your hand, it will start to melt. Heat energy passes from your hand to the ice cube. The heat energy makes the molecules in the ice move faster. The ice begins to melt, or become a liquid.

Heat energy can be passed in three ways. One way is by **conduction.** Heat passes through solids by conduction. When one object passes heat to another by conduction, the heat keeps flowing until both objects are equally hot.

Have you ever eaten hot soup with a metal spoon? After a while, the spoon gets hot. The hot soup causes the molecules in the spoon to move faster. The heat travels from the soup up the spoon to your hand.

Convection is the way heat passes through liquids and gases. Molecules in liquids and gases move apart when they are heated. This happens during convection. When you heat water on the stove, the bottom layer of water is heated first. The molecules in this layer of water move farther apart. This layer floats to the top, and the cooler, heavier water on top falls to the bottom. These movements are called **convection currents.** In winter, convection heats the air in your house.

The third way of passing heat energy is by **radiation.** Radiation moves in waves. Solar heat comes to you in radiation waves.

A. Fill in the missing words.

1. Heat energy is energy passed as _____ from one object to another. (heat, wind)

2. In winter, _____ heats the air in your house. (convection, radiation)

3. Heat energy can be passed in _____ ways. (three, ten)

4. Heat passes through solids by _____. (convection, conduction)

B. Answer <u>True</u> or <u>False</u>.

1. Heat passes from a cooler object to a hotter object. _____

2. In convection, heat is passed by movements called convection currents. _____

3. Solar heat comes to you in radiation waves. _____

4. Molecules in liquids and gases move apart when they are heated. _____

C. Use the words below to complete the sentences. You will use each word twice.

| conduction | convection | radiation |

1. Solar heat comes to you in _____ waves.

2. When one object passes heat to another by _____, the heat keeps flowing until both objects are equally hot.

3. When you heat water on the stove, heat is passed by _____ currents.

4. A spoon in hot soup is heated by _____.

5. The passing of heat energy in waves is _____.

6. In winter, the air in your house is heated by _____.

Wind Energy

Sailboats are powered by wind energy.

Windmills use wind energy to make electricity.

Wind is caused by heat from the sun. The sun heats air by convection. The convection currents that move through heated water also move through heated air. The moving air is called wind.

The sun warms the surface of Earth. Some parts of Earth's surface, such as roads and beaches, absorb, or take in, more heat than others. The air over these areas becomes warmer than the air around them. This warm air rises, and the cool air around it moves in to take its place. This convection current happens anywhere that air becomes heated. Sometimes the air moves slowly. You cannot feel the wind at all. Sometimes it moves fast.

Wind is a source of mechanical energy. Any matter that is moving is using mechanical energy. The wind can move things. A very strong wind can push over trees and buildings.

One of the ways people first used **wind energy** was to power sailboats. As the wind pushes against the sails, it moves the boat across the water. Windmills are another way people use wind energy. A windmill has flat blades on a wheel. Wind pushes the blades and makes the wheel turn. The energy of the turning wheel can be used to pump water from a well. It can also be used to make electricity. People have been using windmills for more than a thousand years.

A. Fill in the missing words.

1. Wind is caused by heat from the _____. (sun, oceans)

2. A _____ current happens anywhere that air becomes heated. (conduction, convection)

3. Some parts of Earth's surface, such as _____, absorb more heat than others. (beaches, mountains)

4. Warm air rises, and _____ air around it moves in to take its place. (fast, cool)

5. _____ air is wind. (Hot, Moving)

6. Wind is a source of _____ energy. (mechanical, heat)

7. _____ are a way people use wind energy. (Radios, Windmills)

8. People have been using windmills for _____ years. (more than a thousand, ten)

B. Answer True or False.

1. Moving air is called wind. _____

2. The sun heats air by convection. _____

3. Cool air rises, and the warm air around it moves in to take its place. _____

4. Sailboats use electrical energy. _____

5. Air always moves slowly. _____

6. Wind is a source of mechanical energy. ___

C. Answer the questions.

1. What causes wind? _____

_____

2. Name two ways people use wind energy. _____

_____

Water Energy

A Waterwheel

Hoover Dam

Moving water can push on objects and move them. Remember that any matter that is moving is using mechanical energy. So water is a source of mechanical energy. The energy that comes from the push of water is **water energy.**

A long time ago, people learned to use water energy for waterwheels. Waterwheels are built on streams. A waterwheel is a large wheel with blades on it. As water pushes on the blades, the wheel turns. Even today, energy from waterwheels is used to grind grain and to cut logs.

When water falls from a high place to a lower place, it carries a lot of energy. Dams are built on rivers and lakes to make use of this energy. Dams hold back a great amount of water. This water is sent through pipes to **water turbines** hundreds of feet below. A turbine is like a waterwheel, but it turns much faster. The falling water turns the turbines. The water energy that the turbines collect is then used to run a **generator.** The generator makes electricity.

A lot of electricity can be made by dams. The Hoover Dam, on the border between Arizona and Nevada, is one of the highest dams in the world. It sends electricity to Arizona, California, and Nevada.

Water is a good source of energy. It does not pollute the air. It will never run out. But water power plants can be built only near a waterfall or a dam. Also, dams cost a great deal of money to build. All energy cannot come from water energy.

A. Use the words below to complete the sentences.

dam	generator	water
electricity	mechanical	waterwheels
energy	turbine	wind

1. Any matter that is moving is using _____ energy.

2. The energy that comes from the push of _____ is water energy.

3. A long time ago, people learned to use water energy for

   _____.

4. When water falls from a high place to a lower place, it carries a

   lot of _____.

5. A _____ is like a waterwheel.

6. Water energy that a turbine collects is used to run a

   _____.

7. A generator makes _____.

8. Water power plants can be built only near a waterfall or

   a _____.

B. The sentences below tell how falling water makes electricity. Number the sentences in the correct order. The first one is done for you.

_____ Water turns the turbines.

___1___ The dam holds back water.

_____ Water energy that the turbines collect runs a generator.

_____ The generator makes electricity.

_____ Water is sent through pipes to water turbines hundreds of feet below.

Steam Energy

Turbine Wheels

Steam Goes In

Steam Changes to Water

Steam Turbine Operating a Ship's Propeller

When water boils, it turns into a gas. This gas is called **steam.** Steam can push on objects and move them. Any matter that is moving is using mechanical energy. Steam is a source of mechanical energy. The energy that comes from the push of steam is **steam energy.**

Steam is made in a boiler. A boiler has a large tank and a furnace. The tank holds water, and the furnace burns fuel to heat the water. Coal, oil, and wood are three kinds of fuel used to produce steam. When the fuel burns, the chemical energy stored in it changes into heat energy. The heat energy heats the water in the boiler and changes it into steam.

You have learned that wind and water can turn wheels with blades. Steam can also turn wheels with blades. This kind of wheel is called a **steam turbine.** The energy from steam turbines can be used in many ways.

Many large ships get their energy from steam engines. The steam turbines on these ships turn the ships' propellers. Propellers make the ships move through the water.

Steam turbines are also used to make electricity. Energy from the turbines is used to run generators, which make electricity. Many large electric power plants have steam turbines.

A. Write the letter for the correct answer.

1. When water boils, it turns into a gas called _____ .
   (a) heat   (b) steam   (c) electricity

2. Steam is made in a _____ .
   (a) boiler   (b) waterwheel   (c) steam turbine

3. When fuel burns, the chemical energy stored in it changes into _____ energy.
   (a) electric   (b) mechanical   (c) heat

4. The energy from steam _____ can be used in many ways.
   (a) turbines   (b) generators   (c) propellers

5. Steam turbines on a ship turn the ship's _____ .
   (a) generators   (b) propellers   (c) furnaces

6. Steam turbines are also used to make _____ .
   (a) fuel   (b) water   (c) electricity

B. Answer True or False.

1. Many large ships get their energy from steam engines. _____

2. Many large electric power plants have steam turbines. _____

3. Steam is a source of mechanical energy. _____

4. Propellers make ships move through the water. _____

5. Steam is a liquid. _____

6. A furnace uses electricity to heat water. _____

7. Energy from steam turbines can be used to run electric generators.

   _____

C. Answer the questions.

1. What are the two parts of a boiler? _____

   _____

2. What are three kinds of fuel used to produce steam? _____

   _____

Nuclear Energy

Nuclear Power Plant

There is energy stored in the nucleus of an atom. You have learned that the nucleus is the center of an atom. The protons and neutrons in the nucleus are held together by a very strong force. Scientists can split the nuclei of some atoms. They fire neutrons at the nuclei at high speeds. When the nuclei split, they give off a large amount of energy. This energy is called **nuclear energy.**

Nuclear energy is produced in **nuclear reactors.** Nuclear reactors have very thick walls. Inside, heat energy from the splitting atoms is used to heat water and make steam. The steam is then used to make electricity.

Nuclear energy does not pollute the air. You might think that nuclear energy is the perfect source of energy. But the atoms that scientists split to make electricity are atoms of the element uranium. There is not much uranium in the world. One day it will all be gone. Also, nuclear energy can be dangerous. Atomic bombs use the energy from splitting atoms.

When an atom splits, it gives off radiation. Radiation can make people very sick. Also, the splitting of atoms leaves behind dangerous wastes. Many people think that nuclear energy is too dangerous to use. Others think that it can be controlled. Today, nuclear energy provides only a small part of the world's energy.

A. Answer True or False.

1. The nucleus is the center of an atom. _____

2. The protons and neutrons in the nucleus are held together by a very weak force. _____

3. The energy given off by the splitting of atomic nuclei is called nuclear energy. _____

4. Nuclear energy is produced in windmills. _____

5. When an atom splits, it gives off radiation. _____

6. Today, nuclear energy provides only a small part of the world's energy. _____

B. Draw lines to complete the sentences.

1. Nuclear energy   is produced in nuclear reactors.

2. Scientists   can make people very sick.

3. Radiation   are held together by a strong force.

4. Protons and neutrons   can split the nuclei of some atoms.

C. Fill in the missing words.

1. There is energy stored in the _____ of an atom. (nucleus, walls)

2. Scientists split nuclei by firing neutrons at them at _____ speeds. (low, high)

3. When the nuclei split, they give off a _____ amount of energy. (small, large)

4. Nuclear energy _____ pollute the air. (does not, does)

5. When an atom splits, it gives off _____. (steam, radiation)

6. Radiation can make people very _____. (sick, healthy)

49

Our Energy Needs

Burning fuels give off smoke.

Fuels such as gasoline will not last forever.

Americans use much more energy than people in other countries. Most Americans have cars, TVs, radios, and many other things that use energy. Many Americans also waste energy. They leave lights and radios on when they are not using them. It is important not to waste energy.

Most of the energy Americans use is from fuels, such as coal, oil, and gasoline. When these fuels are burned, they give off smoke. The smoke pollutes the air. There is another problem with these fuels. They will not last forever.

Today people are trying to find better ways to use energy from wind, water, and the sun. These sources of energy are clean. They will last forever. People are also trying to conserve energy. If everyone works to find better sources of energy and use less of it, there will be plenty of energy for the future.

Underline the correct words.

1. Americans use much more (energy, smoke) than people in other countries.

2. Most of the energy Americans use is from (waste, fuels), such as coal, oil, and gasoline.

3. Smoke (cleans, pollutes) the air.

4. People are trying to (conserve, burn) energy.

Part A

Write the letter for the correct answer.

1. Whenever anything moves, it is using _____ energy.
    (a) mechanical   (b) heat   (c) chemical

2. All the energy in the world comes from _____.
    (a) plants   (b) coal   (c) the sun

3. Heat energy always passes from a _____ object to a cooler object.
    (a) smaller   (b) hotter   (c) larger

4. _____ is caused by convection currents.
    (a) Wind   (b) Steam   (c) Heat

5. Dams are built on rivers and lakes to make use of _____ energy.
    (a) wind   (b) electric   (c) water

6. The energy given off when the nuclei of atoms split is _____.
    (a) solar energy   (b) electric energy   (c) nuclear energy

7. Today people are trying to find better ways to use energy from wind, water, and _____.
    (a) the sun   (b) the moon   (c) oil

Part B

Draw lines to complete the sentences.

1. Mechanical energy   is the energy that comes from the push of water.

2. Heat energy   changes into the other kinds of energy.

3. Water energy   is used by any matter that is moving.

4. Solar energy   is passed as heat from one object to another.

5. Wind energy   is given off when the nucleus of an atom splits.

6. Nuclear energy   comes from moving air.

Fill in the circle in front of the word or phrase that best completes the sentences. The first one is done for you.

1. When water boils, it turns into a gas called
   - ⓐ heat.
   - ● steam.
   - ⓒ energy.

2. When an atom splits, it gives off
   - ⓐ radiation.
   - ⓑ convection.
   - ⓒ carbon dioxide.

3. Wind energy is a source of
   - ⓐ water energy.
   - ⓑ chemical energy.
   - ⓒ mechanical energy.

4. Energy is the ability to
   - ⓐ smell.
   - ⓑ do work.
   - ⓒ see.

5. Many large electric power plants have
   - ⓐ steam turbines.
   - ⓑ windmills.
   - ⓒ propellers.

6. The different kinds of energy come from
   - ⓐ mechanical energy.
   - ⓑ wind.
   - ⓒ solar energy.

7. Coal and oil are kinds of
   - ⓐ fuel.
   - ⓑ plants.
   - ⓒ generators.

8. Energy from the sun is called
   - ⓐ heat energy.
   - ⓑ chemical energy.
   - ⓒ solar energy.

9. Moving water can push on objects and
   - ⓐ burn them.
   - ⓑ move them.
   - ⓒ heat them.

10. The energy given off when the nuclei of atoms split is
    - ⓐ heat energy.
    - ⓑ mechanical energy.
    - ⓒ nuclear energy.

Just for Fun

Each sentence below is about a source of energy. But one word in each sentence is scrambled. Unscramble the letters. Then write the correct word on the lines at the right. Choose from the words below. The first one is done for you.

atom	gasoline	oil	steam
electric	live	radiation	water
energy	nuclear	rivers	years

1. METSA is made in a boiler. S T E A M

2. Someday the supply of coal, LIO, and gasoline will run out. _ _ _

3. Nothing on Earth could IVLE without the sun. _ _ _ _

4. When the nucleus of an MOTA splits, it gives off a very large amount of energy. _ _ _ _

5. Dams are built on SERVIR and lakes. _ _ _ _ _ _

6. Many large CRILETEC power plants have steam turbines. _ _ _ _ _ _ _ _

7. Many people think that RENCULA energy is too dangerous to use. _ _ _ _ _ _ _

8. There are several kinds of YENGER. _ _ _ _ _ _

9. Heat from the sun comes to you in TORADINIA waves. _ _ _ _ _ _ _ _ _

10. NIGOLASE has chemical energy stored in it. _ _ _ _ _ _ _ _

11. Coal and oil were formed from plants and animals millions of RESAY ago. _ _ _ _ _

Solve the Secret Message. Find the first letters of all the words that you unscrambled and write them in order on the lines below.

Secret Message: The most important kind of energy is

_ _ _ _ _ _ _ _ _ _ _ .
1 2 3 4 5 6 7 8 9 10 11

53

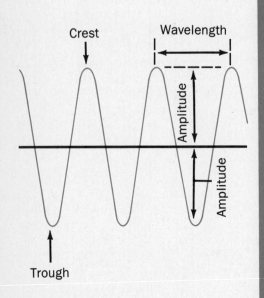

Crest   Wavelength

Amplitude

Amplitude

Trough

Sound Waves

Have you ever thrown a rock into a lake or pond? Small waves move outward in a circle away from the place where the rock hit the water. Some kinds of energy move in waves like these. Sound is a kind of energy that moves in waves. Sound waves can move through all kinds of matter. You cannot see sound waves. But you know they are there because you can hear the sound.

All sounds are made by vibrating objects. To vibrate means to move quickly back and forth. When a vibrating object moves outward, it pushes the air molecules close together. Then they spread out again and push the molecules next to them. This movement of molecules is a sound wave. Sound waves, like waves in a pond, move outward in circles from their source.

Sound waves move more quickly through dense matter. The molecules of dense matter are close together. Sound travels faster through water than through air. This is because the molecules in water are much closer than the molecules in air.

Scientists use special words to describe waves. The highest part of a wave is called the **crest.** The lowest part of a wave is the **trough.** One half the distance between a wave's crest and its trough is the wave's **amplitude.** The **wavelength** of a sound is the distance between the crests of two of its waves. The number of waves that move past one spot in a second is the sound's **frequency.**

A. Underline the correct words.

1. Sound is a kind of energy that moves in (waves, space).

2. Sound waves (cannot, can) move through all kinds of matter.

3. All sounds are made by (still, vibrating) objects.

4. Sound waves, like waves in a pond, move (inward, outward) in circles from their source.

5. Sound waves move more quickly through (dense, light) matter.

6. The lowest part of a wave is the (crest, trough).

B. Draw lines to match the parts of waves with their descriptions.

1. crest | half the distance between a wave's crest and its trough

2. trough | the highest part of a wave

3. amplitude | number of waves that move past one spot in a second

4. wavelength | the lowest part of a wave

5. frequency | the distance between two crests

C. Answer <u>True</u> or <u>False</u>.

1. Energy does not move in waves. _____

2. Sound waves cannot move through matter. _____

3. You cannot see sound waves. _____

4. All sounds are made by vibrating objects. _____

5. Sound waves move outward in circles from the person hearing the sound. _____

6. Sound waves move more quickly through dense matter. _____

7. The molecules of dense matter are far apart. _____

8. The wavelength of a sound is the distance between the crests of two of its waves. _____

Pitch and Loudness

High-Pitched Soft Sound

High-Pitched Loud Sound

Low-Pitched Soft Sound

Low-Pitched Loud Sound

You have learned that all sounds are waves that move through the air. But not all sounds are alike. Some sounds, such as a bird singing, are high sounds. Other sounds, such as a frog croaking, are low sounds. Some sounds are so quiet you can barely hear them. Other sounds are very loud. What makes these sounds different?

The quality of being high or low is a sound's **pitch.** A sound's pitch is the same as the frequency of its sound waves. You have learned that a sound's frequency is the number of waves that move past one spot in a second.

Waves with a high frequency have a high sound. These waves have short wavelengths. Waves with a low frequency have a low sound. These waves have long wavelengths.

A sound's loudness is different from its pitch. A high-pitched sound can be loud or soft. So can a low-pitched sound.

A sound's loudness is the same as the amplitude of its sound waves. You have learned that a wave's amplitude is one half the distance between its crest and its trough. Soft sounds have a low amplitude. Loud sounds have a high amplitude. Look at the pictures on this page to see the difference between high, low, loud, and soft sound waves.

A. Use the words below to complete the sentences.

amplitude	Loud	pitch
frequency	loudness	Soft
high	low	

1. The quality of being high or low is a sound's _____.

2. A sound's pitch is the same as the _____ of its sound waves.

3. Waves with a high frequency have a _____ sound.

4. Waves with a low frequency have a _____ sound.

5. A sound's _____ is different from its pitch.

6. A sound's loudness is the same as the _____ of its sound waves.

7. _____ sounds have a low amplitude.

8. _____ sounds have a high amplitude.

B. Answer the questions.

1. What is a sound's pitch? _____

_____

2. What is a sound's frequency? _____

_____

_____

C. Answer True or False.

1. All sounds are waves that move through the air. _____

2. Waves with a high frequency have a high sound. _____

3. A sound's loudness is the same as its pitch. _____

57

Saxophone

Guitar

Cymbals

The sounds that you hear can be divided into music and noise. What is the difference? Music is pleasant to listen to. Noise is not. Music is made of notes, or sounds with a certain pitch. These sounds have certain frequencies. Noise is made of sounds with different frequencies.

In music, each note lasts for a certain amount of time. The times that the different notes last make up a pattern. This pattern is the music's rhythm. Noise does not have rhythm.

When people sing, they make music with their voices. People also make music with instruments. The three main kinds are **wind, stringed,** and **percussion** instruments.

One kind of wind instrument, such as the saxophone, has a thin piece of wood called a reed that vibrates. The person playing the instrument blows into the mouthpiece, which has the reed attached to it. The vibrating reed makes the column of air inside the instrument vibrate.

The piano, the guitar, and the violin are stringed instruments. They make sounds by vibrating strings. The strings are hit by tiny hammers, plucked with the fingers, or moved with a bow. The vibrating strings cause the air around them to vibrate.

Percussion instruments, such as drums and cymbals, make sounds by being struck. When the instrument is struck, it vibrates and causes the air around it to vibrate. Most percussion instruments do not have any certain pitch. Instead, they mark the beat of the music.

A. Answer <u>True</u> or <u>False</u>.

1. Music is pleasant to listen to. _____

2. Music is made of notes. _____

3. Noise is made of sounds with the same frequencies. _____

4. Noise is rhythm. _____

5. When people sing, they make music with their voices. _____

6. The piano is a wind instrument. _____

7. Percussion instruments make sounds by vibrating strings. _____

8. Stringed instruments make sounds by vibrating strings. _____

9. Stringed instruments can make only noise. _____

B. Choose the instrument that matches the type of instrument and write its name in the blank.

drums	guitar	saxophone

1. stringed instrument _____

2. wind instrument _____

3. percussion instrument _____

C. Answer the question.

What are two reasons why music is different from noise? _____

_____

_____

_____

_____

How You Hear

Outer Ear   Middle Ear   Inner Ear

Small Bones

Auditory Nerve

Auditory Canal

Eardrum

The Parts of the Ear

You hear many different sounds every day. You hear people talking. You hear music and the sounds of cars. You have learned that sound is caused by vibrations. Vibrations send sound waves through the air. But how do your ears turn these sound waves into the sounds you hear?

Your ear has three main parts. They are the outer ear, the middle ear, and the inner ear. The outside part of your ear catches sound waves moving through the air. Then the waves move down the **auditory canal.** You can see the opening of the auditory canal in the middle of your outer ear. The outside part of your ear and the auditory canal are both part of the outer ear.

Sound waves move down the auditory canal to the **eardrum.** The eardrum is a thin piece of skin across the auditory canal. Sound waves make the eardrum vibrate. The vibrations from the eardrum are passed on to three small bones in the middle ear. The bones make the vibrations larger.

The inner ear is filled with liquid. The vibrations from the bones in the middle ear make the liquid move. The moving liquid bends tiny hairs in your inner ear. Your **auditory nerves** feel these hairs move. The auditory nerves turn these movements into signals and send them to the brain. These signals are the sounds you hear.

A. The steps below describe how you hear. Number the steps in the correct order. The first one is done for you.

_____ The sound waves make the eardrum vibrate.

_____ The moving liquid bends tiny hairs in your inner ear.

___1___ The outside part of your ear catches the sound waves moving through the air.

_____ The auditory nerves turn the movements of the tiny hairs into signals and send them to the brain.

_____ The sound waves move down the auditory canal.

_____ The vibrations from the small bones in your middle ear make the liquid in your inner ear move.

_____ Vibrations from the eardrum are passed to small bones.

B. Underline the correct words.

1. The outside part of your ear and the auditory canal are both part of the (outer, inner) ear.

2. The three small bones in the middle ear make the vibrations (smaller, larger).

3. The inner ear is filled with (liquid, air).

4. Sound waves move down the auditory canal to the (eardrum, outer ear).

5. The auditory nerves send signals to the (brain, eardrum).

6. Your (inner, middle) ear has three small bones.

7. Your ear has (six, three) main parts.

C. Name the three parts of the ear.

1. _____

2. _____

3. _____

61

How You Talk

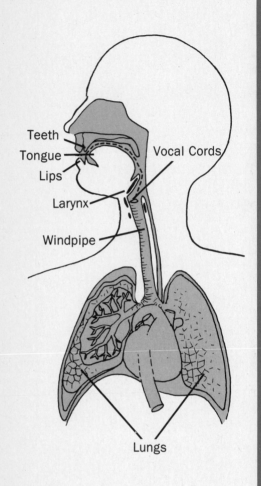

Teeth
Tongue
Lips
Larynx
Windpipe
Vocal Cords
Lungs

Parts of the Mouth and Throat

You have learned that all sounds are vibrations. When you speak, you send vibrations out into the air. Where do these vibrations come from?

Your voice begins in your **larynx,** or voice box. The voice box is the top part of your **windpipe.** Your **vocal cords** are small bands of tissue on either side of your voice box.

When you breathe, the vocal cords are relaxed. Your windpipe is completely open. When you talk, the muscles in your larynx pull on your vocal cords. The muscles pull the vocal cords over your windpipe. Only a narrow opening is left. The air coming up through your windpipe makes the vocal cords vibrate. These vibrations are sounds. When you talk, you use your mouth, tongue, teeth, and lips to shape these sounds into words.

Everyone talks the same way. But you can recognize the voices of people you know. This is because no two people have voices that sound exactly alike. Everyone's voice has its own pitch and its own sound.

The pitch of a person's voice depends on how large his or her voice box is. The larger a person's voice box is, the longer his or her vocal cords are. People with high voices have small voice boxes and short vocal cords. People with deep voices have large voice boxes and long vocal cords. People use their teeth, tongue, and lips differently when they talk. This is another reason why no two human voices sound exactly alike.

A. **Fill in the missing words.**

1. Your voice begins in your _____. (larynx, mouth)

2. Your vocal cords are small bands of tissue on either side of your _____. (voice box, mouth)

3. Air coming up through your windpipe makes your vocal cords _____. (relax, vibrate)

4. People with high voices have _____ vocal cords. (short, long)

5. People with low voices have _____ vocal cords. (short, long)

B. **Answer True or False.**

1. Your vocal cords are small bands of tissue on either side of your voice box. _____

2. When you breathe, your vocal cords are tight. _____

3. When you talk, your vocal cords are relaxed. _____

4. No two human voices sound exactly alike. _____

5. Everyone's voice has the same pitch and the same sound. _____

6. People with deep voices have large voice boxes and long vocal cords. _____

7. People use their teeth, tongue, and lips differently when they talk. _____

8. Your voice begins in your tongue. _____

C. **Use each word to write a sentence about how you talk.**

1. larynx _____

_____

2. vocal cords _____

_____

How Light Rays Bend

This girl can see her reflection in the mirror.

Light is a kind of energy. Light is given off in tiny particles called **photons.** Photons have no mass. They are not matter. Photons travel in waves. Most light waves have so many photons that the separate photons cannot be seen. They look like solid waves of light.

Sound waves are movements of the matter through which they travel. So sound waves can travel only through matter. But light waves are waves of photons. So light waves can travel through empty space.

Light travels very quickly. It goes through 186,225 miles of air in 1 second. Light travels much faster than sound. Sound goes only about one fifth of a mile in a second. Have you ever been in a thunderstorm? If you have, you may remember that you saw lightning a moment before you heard the thunder. The light from the lightning reached you more quickly than the sound did.

Light travels in straight lines called **rays.** When light rays hit a smooth, shiny surface such as a mirror, they bounce back. You see whatever is in front of the surface. This is called **reflection.**

Light rays cannot turn corners. But they can be bent by things in their path. When a light ray goes through a different substance, such as glass or water, it changes direction. Then the ray comes out on the other side and goes straight on. This is called **refraction.** Look at the picture of a straw in a glass of water. The straw is not really bent. The light rays that your eyes see are bent.

A. Use the words below to complete the sentences.

energy	matter	space
mass	photons	wave

Light is a kind of _____. Light is given off in tiny particles

called _____. Photons have no _____. They are not

_____. Photons travel in _____.

B. Write the letter for the correct answer.

1. Sound waves can travel only through _____.
   (a) space   (b) water   (c) matter

2. Light travels much _____ than sound.
   (a) faster   (b) more slowly   (c) more loudly

3. Light travels in straight lines called _____.
   (a) particles   (b) rays   (c) photons

4. The bending of light rays by things in their path is called _____.
   (a) refraction   (b) reflection   (c) transmission

5. When light rays hit a smooth, shiny surface and bounce back, it is

   called _____.
   (a) transmission   (b) refraction   (c) reflection

6. Light is given off in tiny particles called _____.
   (a) electrons   (b) photons   (c) straws

C. Answer True or False.

1. Photons have mass. _____

2. Photons travel in waves. _____

3. Light goes only about one mile in a second. _____

4. Light is much faster than sound. _____

5. Light rays cannot turn corners. _____

Sources of Light

Daytime

Nighttime

How the Sun Lights Earth

Most of the light on Earth comes from the sun. The sun shines during the daytime. At night, the sun sets and it is dark. Why does the sun shine only during the day?

The sun is always shining. But because Earth **rotates,** or spins around, you see the sun's light only during the day. When the part of Earth where you are is facing the sun, sunlight falls on it. But as Earth spins, your part of Earth moves and faces away from the sun. Then it is night. Your nighttime is daytime for the people on the other side of Earth.

At night, some light comes from the moon. The moon does not really give off its own light. It just reflects light from the sun. So moonlight is very dim.

Most of the people in the world use electric light bulbs to see at night. The light from a light bulb comes from the **filament.** The filament is a small piece of tungsten wire. Electricity passes through the wire and makes it very hot. The hot wire gives off light.

Fill in the missing words.

1. Most of the light on Earth comes from the _____. (sun, moon)

2. Because Earth _____, you see the sun's light only during the day. (is round, rotates)

3. Your nighttime is _____ for the people on the other side of Earth. (twilight, daytime)

4. The moon reflects light from _____. (the sun, Earth)

5. Moonlight is very _____. (bright, dim)

Color

Every day, you see objects of many different colors. The objects do not really have colors. The colors come from light. An object has a certain color because of the way it absorbs light.

Sunlight is a mixture of light of all colors. Each color of light has a different wavelength. The photons of different colors have different energies. Red light has a long wavelength and low-energy photons. Violet light has a short wavelength and high-energy photons.

A red object, such as an apple, absorbs all colors of light except red. The red light is reflected. You see a red apple. White objects reflect all colors of light. Black objects absorb all colors of light.

The **spectrum** is all the colors of light. You can see the spectrum by using a **prism.** A prism is a piece of glass shaped like a triangle. When light passes through the prism, it is separated into all its different colors. The spectrum can also be seen in a rainbow. Rainbows happen when the sun shines after it has been raining. The drops of water in the sky act like tiny prisms to separate out the different colors of sunlight.

The different colors of light can be seen in a rainbow.

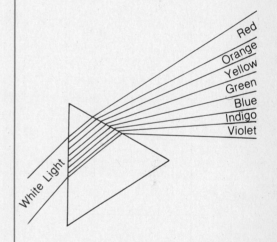

When light passes through a prism, it is separated into its different colors.

Answer True or False.

1. An object has a certain color because of the way it absorbs light.

   _____

2. Sunlight is made of only one color of light. _____

3. A red object reflects all colors of light except red. _____

Lenses

Convex Lens

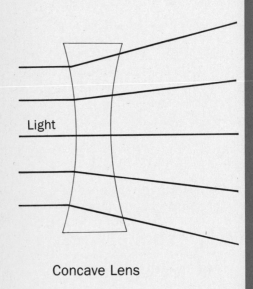

Concave Lens

You know that light can be refracted, or bent. **Lenses** are used for bending light. They can make objects look smaller or larger. They can make things that are far away look close. How do lenses work?

Lenses are made of glass or other materials that light can pass through. The two main kinds of lenses are **concave** lenses and **convex** lenses. A concave lens is thinner in the middle than it is at the edges. A concave lens bends light rays so that they spread apart. A convex lens is thicker in the middle than it is at the edges. A convex lens bends light rays so that they come together.

Lenses have many different uses. People who have trouble seeing wear eyeglasses or contact lenses. Eyeglasses are lenses worn in front of the eyes. Contact lenses are lenses worn on the eye. Contact lenses are made of plastic. Concave lenses help people who have trouble seeing objects in the distance. Convex lenses help people who have trouble seeing objects close to them.

Scientists use lenses in microscopes. The lenses in microscopes make very tiny objects look larger. Scientists use microscopes to study things that are normally too small to see. Scientists also use lenses in telescopes. Telescopes make faraway objects look as if they are closer. Scientists use telescopes to study stars and planets.

Lenses are used in cameras. They **focus** light on the film. Without lenses, there would not be photographs or movies!

A. Use the words below to complete the sentences.

closer	convex	light
concave	focus	microscopes

1. Lenses are used for bending _____ .

2. A _____ lens is thinner in the middle than it is at the edges.

3. A _____ lens is thicker in the middle than it is at the edges.

4. The lenses in _____ make very tiny objects look larger.

5. Telescopes make objects that are very far away look _____ .

6. Lenses used in cameras _____ light on the film.

B. Answer True or False.

1. The main kinds of lenses are concave lenses and convex lenses.

   _____

2. A concave lens bends light rays so that they come together.

   _____

3. A convex lens bends light rays so that they come together.

   _____

4. Lenses are used in cameras. _____

5. Lenses are not used in telescopes. _____

C. Answer the questions.

1. What do telescopes do? _____

   _____

2. What do scientists use telescopes for? _____

   _____

How You See

Retina

Lens

Cornea

Pupil

Iris

Optic Nerve

The Main Parts of the Eye

How do your eyes turn light into what you see? Your **eyeballs** are almost round. They have a thin covering called the **cornea.** The cornea helps to protect your eyes. The black circle in the middle of each of your eyes is the **pupil.** The pupil is a hole. Light goes through the pupil.

The colored part of your eye around the pupil is the **iris.** The iris changes the size of the pupil to let in the right amount of light. When the light is bright, the iris makes the pupil small. When the light is dim, it makes the pupil large.

Light enters the pupil and goes through the lens. The lens bends light rays so they hit the **retina** at the back of the eye. The retina is attached to the **optic nerve.** The optic nerve sends messages to your brain. Your brain sees these messages as pictures.

Draw lines to match each part of the eye with its description.

1. pupil   attached to the optic nerve

2. iris   a hole in the center of the eye

3. lens   sends messages to the brain

4. retina   the colored part around the pupil

5. optic nerve   bends light rays

■ Review

Part A

Underline the correct words.

1. Sound is a kind of energy that moves in (rays, waves).

2. All sounds are made by (vibrating, colored) objects.

3. The lowest part of a wave is called the (crest, trough).

4. The (wavelength, amplitude) of a sound is the distance between the crests of two of its waves.

5. A sound's pitch is the same as the (amplitude, frequency) of its sound waves.

6. Your voice begins in your (larynx, eardrum).

7. Light is given off in tiny particles called (electrons, photons).

8. Light travels much (more slowly, faster) than sound.

9. Light travels in straight lines called (rays, refractions).

10. Because Earth (reflects, rotates), you see the sun's light only during the day.

Part B

Read each sentence. Write <u>True</u> if the sentence is true. Write <u>False</u> if the sentence is false.

1. Sound waves can move through all kinds of matter. _____

2. Sound waves move outward in squares from their source. _____

3. A sound's loudness is the same as the amplitude of its sound waves. _____

4. Noise is made of notes. _____

5. The moon gives off its own light. _____

6. The light from a bulb comes from the filament. _____

7. An object that absorbs all colors of light is red. _____

Fill in the circle in front of the word or phrase that best completes the sentences. The first one is done for you.

1. Sound waves move more quickly through matter that is
   ⓐ colored.
   ● dense.
   ⓒ light.

2. Sound waves with a high frequency have a
   ⓐ loud sound.
   ⓑ low sound.
   ⓒ high sound.

3. Most percussion instruments do not have any certain
   ⓐ pitch.
   ⓑ beat.
   ⓒ vibration.

4. The inner ear is filled with
   ⓐ air.
   ⓑ liquid.
   ⓒ gas.

5. The auditory nerves send signals to the
   ⓐ eardrum.
   ⓑ voice box.
   ⓒ brain.

6. Your voice begins in your
   ⓐ larynx.
   ⓑ brain.
   ⓒ auditory canal.

7. When light waves hit a smooth, shiny surface and bounce back, it is called
   ⓐ reflection.
   ⓑ concave.
   ⓒ amplitude.

8. Each color of light has a different
   ⓐ frequency.
   ⓑ wavelength.
   ⓒ cornea.

9. A concave lens bends light rays so that they
   ⓐ change color.
   ⓑ bounce back.
   ⓒ spread apart.

10. The black circle in the middle of your eye is the
   ⓐ pupil.
   ⓑ cornea.
   ⓒ retina.

Use the words below to answer the questions.

bend	energy	music	vocal
crest	iris	pitch	waves
eardrum	lenses	trough	

1. What part of your ear vibrates? _ _ _ _ _ _ _
                                              8

2. What kind of sound is made of notes? _ _ _ _ _
                                            3

3. What is the lowest part of a wave? _ _ _ _ _ _
                                        13   2

4. What is the colored part of your eye? _ _ _ _
                                          10   1

5. What is the same as the frequency of a sound's waves? _ _ _ _ _
                                                              12

6. How do sound and light move? _ _ _ _ _
                                   6

7. What do lenses do to light rays? _ _ _ _
                                      4 5

8. What cords vibrate when you talk? _ _ _ _ _
                                            9

9. What are used in microscopes? _ _ _ _ _ _
                                       7

10. What is light, music or energy? _ _ _ _ _ _
                                          11

Now find the letters that have numbers below them. Write those letters below. When you are finished, you will have the answer to a riddle.

Riddle: What kinds of energy move in waves?

_ _ _ _ _   _ _ _   _ _ _ _ _
1 2 3 4 5   6 7 8   9 10 11 12 13

■ UNIT 5 ▪ Magnetism and Electricity ■
What Is Electricity?

Negative electrons moving from clouds to Earth caused this flash of lightning.

Electricity is an important part of our lives. Electric lights help us see at night. Television gives us entertainment and news. Washers, refrigerators, and telephones make our lives easier.

Electricity is caused by matter that has an electric charge. You know that matter is made of atoms. Atoms are made of protons, neutrons, and electrons. The protons and neutrons are in the nucleus. Protons have a positive electric charge. Neutrons have no charge. So the nucleus has a positive charge. Electrons move around the nucleus. They have a negative charge. Things with opposite electric charges attract each other. So the electrons are attracted to the nucleus.

As long as an atom has the same number of protons and electrons, the atom has no charge. But an atom can lose electrons. When you comb your hair, electrons from your hair may come off onto the comb. Because your hair has lost electrons, it has a positive electric charge. Because the comb has gained electrons, it has a negative electric charge. Your hair and the comb attract each other. Your hair seems to follow the comb into the air.

Electrons can also move from one object to another. During a thunderstorm, tiny particles in clouds can rub together and separate electrons from their atoms. Earth has a positive charge. So the negative electrons move from the cloud to Earth. The moving electrons cause a flash of light. The flash of light is lightning.

A. Answer True or False.

1. Electricity is caused by matter that has an electric charge.

   _____

2. Atoms are not made of any smaller particles. _____

3. The electrons are in the nucleus. _____

4. Things with opposite electric charges attract each other. _____

5. An atom cannot lose electrons. _____

6. Electrons can move from a cloud to Earth. _____

B. Use the words below to complete the sentences.

atoms	matter	particles
Electricity	opposite	same

1. _____ is an important part of our lives.

2. Electricity is caused by _____ that has an electric charge.

3. Matter is made of _____.

4. Things that have _____ charges attract each other.

5. As long as an atom has the _____ number of protons and electrons, it has no charge.

C. Draw lines to match each particle with its description.

1. proton   no electric charge

2. neutron   attracted to a positive charge

3. electron   attracted to a negative charge

D. Name four things that use electricity. _____

_____

_____

75

Electric Currents

Inside an Electric Cord

You have learned that when electrons leave their atoms, matter becomes electrically charged. The charged particles in electrically charged matter usually move in all directions. The movement of charged particles in many directions is called **static electricity.** Electrically charged matter whose particles all move in the same direction is called **current electricity.**

Most of the electricity we use every day is current electricity. Current electricity is made by a generator. The generator gathers electrons. Then it pushes them all in the same direction. It forces electrons to move through a **conductor.**

A conductor is a kind of matter that electrons can move through easily. Metal wire is the conductor we use most to carry electricity. Matter that electrons cannot move through easily is an **insulator.** Rubber is a good insulator. Electric wires are often covered with rubber to keep the electrons moving along in the wire.

There are two kinds of current electricity. **Direct current** happens when the electrons flow in the same direction all the time. Batteries produce direct current electricity. **Alternating current** happens when the electron flow changes directions. The electric outlets in your house provide alternating current electricity.

A. Write the letter for the correct answer.

1. The movement of charged particles in many directions is called
   _____ electricity.
   (a) current   (b) static   (c) regular

2. Electrically charged matter whose particles all move in the same
   direction is called _____ electricity.
   (a) current   (b) static   (c) regular

3. Most of the electricity we use every day is _____ electricity.
   (a) static   (b) regular   (c) current

4. Current electricity is made by a _____ .
   (a) generator   (b) pump   (c) comb

5. A generator forces electrons to move through _____ .
   (a) an insulator   (b) a rope   (c) a conductor

6. Matter that electrons cannot move through easily is _____ .
   (a) a conductor   (b) a metal   (c) an insulator

7. _____ happens when the electron flow changes direction.
   (a) Alternating current   (b) Regular current   (c) Direct current

B. Answer True or False.

1. Rubber is the conductor we use for most of our needs. _____

2. Batteries produce direct current electricity. _____

3. The electric outlets in your house provide direct current electricity.

   _____

4. Alternating current happens when the electrons flow in the same
   direction all the time. _____

5. When electrons leave their atoms, matter becomes electrically
   charged. _____

6. Charged particles moving in many directions is called static
   electricity. _____

Broken insulation is dangerous.

The path taken by an electric current is called an electric **circuit.** Electric current flows from the source of the electricity through a wire. At the end of the wire is something that uses electricity. It may be a bulb in a lamp. The bulb is lighted by the electric current. But an electric circuit must be a two-way path. If the electric charge cannot return to its source, it may build up somewhere along the circuit. If it builds up, the circuit will not work.

Most electric circuits have a switch. When the switch is off, the circuit is open. The current's path is broken. The current cannot get back to its source. When the switch is on, there are no breaks in the path. It is a closed circuit. The current can complete its path.

Sometimes, insulation wrapped around the wires wears out and breaks. Wires that should be kept separate may touch each other. Then electrons can move from wire to wire. They can take a shortcut in the path through the circuit. The shortcut is called a **short circuit.** Short circuits are dangerous. They can start fires.

Electric current is measured in **amperes.** The number of amperes tells how strong the current is. The amount of push a source of electricity gives the electricity is measured in **volts.** The number of volts tells how easily the current can move through the circuit. Some electricity always changes to heat energy. So a source must have enough volts to produce extra electricity.

A. Underline the correct words.

1. The amount of push a source of electricity gives the electricity is measured in (volts, circuits).

2. Short circuits can (increase the number of volts, start fires).

3. When a lamp switch is (on, off), there are no breaks in the path.

4. Electric current is measured in (volts, amperes).

5. The path taken by an electric current is called an electric (source, circuit).

6. When a lamp switch is off, the current's path is (broken, not broken).

B. Use the words below to complete the sentences.

amperes	closed	path
builds	current	short circuit
circuit	open	volts

1. The path taken by an electric current is called an electric

   _____.

2. An electric circuit must be a two-way _____.

3. If an electric charge _____ up somewhere along a circuit, the circuit will not work.

4. When there are no breaks in the path, the circuit is _____.

5. When a switch is off, the circuit is _____.

6. When electrons can move from wire to wire, the shortcut is called

   a _____.

7. The amount of push a source of electricity has is measured in

   _____.

8. Electric current is measured in units called _____.

Fuses and Circuit Breakers

Circuit Breakers

You have learned that when electricity flows through a circuit, some electricity changes into heat. Sometimes too much current goes through a circuit. For instance, lightning can cause too much current in a circuit. When this happens, the device that is using the electricity can break. The wires of the circuit get very hot. The heat can start a fire.

To keep fires from starting, **fuses** are put in circuits. A fuse is like a little light bulb. It has a wire inside that melts easily. When the circuit has too much current, the wire heats up. The wire becomes so hot that it melts. The circuit is broken. The current cannot complete its path. The path is an open circuit. No more electricity can flow through it.

Every circuit usually has its own fuse. When a fuse breaks a circuit, a fresh fuse must be put in the place of the burned-out fuse. Otherwise the circuit will not work.

Circuit breakers are sometimes used instead of fuses. A circuit breaker has a switch that works like a fuse. If the electric current is too great, a switch opens and stops the current. When a circuit breaker breaks a circuit, it does not have to be replaced. The switch can be closed, and the circuit will work again.

Without fuses and circuit breakers, people would have no way of knowing if there were too much current in a circuit. There would be many more fires started by electricity. Fuses and circuit breakers help make electricity safe to use.

A. Answer True or False.

1. When electricity flows through a circuit, some electricity changes into heat. _____

2. If a circuit is open, the current can complete its path. _____

3. When a fuse breaks a circuit, a fresh fuse must be put in the place of the burned-out fuse. _____

4. A circuit breaker has a switch that works like a fuse. _____

5. When a circuit breaker breaks a circuit, it has to be replaced. _____

B. Use the words below to complete the sentences.

breakers	fuse	lightning
circuit	heat	safe

1. _____ can cause too much current in a circuit.

2. A _____ is like a little light bulb.

3. Every _____ usually has its own fuse.

4. Circuit _____ are sometimes used instead of fuses.

5. Fuses and circuit breakers help make electricity _____ to use.

C. Write the letter for the correct answer.

1. When electricity flows through a circuit, some electricity changes into _____.
   (a) steam   (b) heat   (c) smoke

2. When there is too much current in a circuit, the wires of the circuit get very _____.
   (a) hot   (b) cool   (c) hard

Dry Cell

A Battery for a Car

If you have a television set at home, it is easy to make it work. You just plug the end of the electric cord into an outlet and turn on the TV. The electric current you need comes from the outlets in your home.

But when you are away from home, there may not be electric outlets around. Where do you get electricity to run your radio or your flashlight? **Dry cells** and **batteries** store electricity. If you have a dry cell or a battery, you can take electric energy with you wherever you go.

Dry cells are not really dry. The outside of one kind of dry cell is made of the metal zinc. Inside the cell is a paste of chemicals. The chemicals react with the zinc, which loses some electrons. As the chemicals react, a flow of electrons forms an electric current. So chemical energy becomes electric energy.

A dry cell has two posts called **terminals.** One terminal is positive. The other is negative. A wire can be put between the terminals to make a circuit. You can make something that uses electricity, such as a light bulb, a part of the circuit. The flow of electric current will light the bulb.

A battery is two or more dry cells working together. A battery can give more volts than a dry cell. The more cells in a battery, the more volts it can give. A battery is used in most cars. The battery itself does not make the car run. The engine makes the car run. But the battery gives the current to start the engine.

A. Write the letter for the correct answer.

1. Dry cells and batteries store _____ .
   (a) electricity   (b) mechanical energy   (c) outlets

2. Inside a dry cell is a paste of _____ .
   (a) metals   (b) batteries   (c) chemicals

3. Chemicals in dry cells react with zinc to make _____ .
   (a) terminals   (b) electricity   (c) more dry cells

4. A dry cell has two posts called _____ .
   (a) outlets   (b) electric currents   (c) terminals

5. A battery is two or more _____ working together.
   (a) terminals   (b) dry cells   (c) volts

6. A battery in a car gives the current to _____ .
   (a) make the car run   (b) ring a bell   (c) start the engine

B. Use each word to write a sentence about dry cells and batteries.

1. terminals _____

   _____

2. volts _____

   _____

C. Answer True or False.

1. At home, the electric current you need comes from outlets.

   _____

2. Dry cells are really dry. _____

3. A wire can be put between the terminals of a dry cell to make a

   circuit. _____

4. A dry cell can give more volts than a battery. _____

5. One terminal of a dry cell is positive and the other is negative.

   _____

What Is Magnetism?

Different poles attract, and the same poles repel.

What keeps a refrigerator door closed? Most refrigerator doors are kept closed by **magnetism.** Magnetism is a pulling force that certain metals have. These metals, called **magnets,** attract and repel other pieces of metal. Attract means that two objects pull toward each other. Repel means that two objects push away from each other.

All magnets have two ends called **poles.** Each magnet has a north pole and a south pole. The north pole of one magnet attracts the south pole of another magnet. But the north pole of one magnet repels the north pole of another magnet. Two south poles also repel each other.

In some ways, Earth acts like a magnet with two poles. You can tell by using a magnetic compass. A magnetic compass is an instrument with a magnetized needle. One end of the needle always points to the magnetic north pole of Earth. Sailors use compasses to tell what direction they are going.

Magnets do not have to touch a piece of metal to attract it. There is an attracting area around every magnet called the **magnetic field.** When a piece of metal comes near a magnet, it is attracted by the magnetic field. The attraction gets stronger as the metal gets closer to the magnet.

A. Draw >—< to show when two magnetic poles attract. Draw <—> to show when two magnetic poles repel.

1. north pole _____ south pole

2. south pole _____ south pole

3. south pole _____ north pole

4. north pole _____ north pole

B. Use the words below to complete the sentences.

Attract	Magnetism	Repel
compass	metal	stronger
magnetic field	poles	weaker

1. _____ is a pulling force that certain metals have.

2. Magnets attract and repel other pieces of _____.

3. _____ means that two objects push away from each other.

4. _____ means that two objects pull toward each other.

5. All magnets have two ends called _____.

6. You can tell that Earth acts like a magnet by using a magnetic

_____.

7. There is an attracting area around magnets called the

_____.

8. The attraction of a piece of metal gets _____ as the metal gets closer to the magnet.

C. Answer the question.

What is magnetism? _____

_____

Electromagnets

As long as the electricity is turned on, an electromagnet can lift tons of metal.

You have learned that a magnet has a magnetic field around it. This field is the area in which the magnet acts on other objects. Magnetism is related to electricity. When electricity flows through a wire, it makes a magnetic field around the wire.

Suppose an electric wire is bent into a coil. When electricity flows through the wire, a magnetic field forms around the whole coil. The coil becomes a kind of magnet. It has north and south poles, just like a magnet.

If an iron bar is placed inside a coil of wire when electricity flows through it, an **electromagnet** is formed. An electromagnet is a much more powerful magnet than a coil of wire alone. When more wire is looped around the iron, the electromagnet becomes even stronger.

Doorbells are made from a tiny electromagnet. A large electromagnet is so powerful it can lift tons of iron. It can lift cars in junkyards, and even trains. But as soon as the flow of electricity is turned off, an electromagnet loses its magnetism. Then it drops whatever it was holding.

Not only can electricity make magnetic fields, magnetic fields can make electricity. If a magnet is moved in and out of a coil of copper wire, electricity begins to flow through the coil. This way of making electricity is called **electromagnetic induction.** Generators, which supply electricity, make their electricity by electromagnetic induction.

A. **Answer True or False.**

1. Magnetic fields can make electricity. _____

2. Electricity cannot make magnetic fields. _____

3. As soon as the flow of electricity is turned off, an electromagnet gets stronger. _____

4. If a magnet is moved in and out of a coil of copper wire, electricity begins to flow through the coil. _____

B. **Fill in the missing words.**

1. Magnetism is related to _____. (electricity, fuses)

2. A magnet has a magnetic field _____ it. (inside, around)

3. When electricity flows through a wire, _____ forms around the wire. (electromagnetic induction, a magnetic field)

4. If an electric wire is bent into a _____, and electricity flows through it, the coil becomes a kind of magnet. (square, coil)

5. If an iron bar is placed inside a coil of wire when electricity flows through it, _____ is formed. (an electromagnet, a wire)

6. An electromagnet is a much _____ powerful magnet than a coil of wire alone. (more, less)

7. Generators make electricity by _____. (electromagnetic induction, magnets)

C. **Use each pair of words to write a sentence about electromagnets.**

1. iron bar _____

_____

2. copper coil _____

_____

This printing press is run by an electric motor.

Whether you know it or not, there are electric motors all over your home. Electric motors are in clocks, in hair dryers, and in record players. They are in air conditioners, refrigerators, and washing machines. Outside your home, there are much bigger electric motors in many kinds of machines, such as trains and printing presses.

What is an electric motor? An electric motor is a machine that changes electric energy into mechanical energy. As you know, mechanical energy is needed to make anything move.

Electric motors use electromagnets and regular magnets. An electric current passed through the electromagnet keeps changing directions. This makes the poles of the electromagnet change. The north pole becomes the south pole, and the south pole becomes the north pole. Because of this change, its north pole is always lined up with the north pole of the regular magnet. The two north poles repel, making the electromagnet keep turning. As the electromagnet turns, it turns a rod that can run a machine. Belts can be attached to the rod. The belts can move machine parts.

In today's world, it would be difficult to find a machine that is not run by an electric motor. Even an electrically run generator that makes electricity and supplies it to a large area needs an electric motor to keep working.

A. Make a list of six machines that are run by electric motors.

_____

_____

_____

_____

B. Fill in the missing words.

1. An electric motor is a machine that changes electric energy into

   _____ energy. (mechanical, solar)

2. _____ energy is needed to make anything move.
   (Motor, Mechanical)

3. Electric motors use electromagnets and _____.
   (regular magnets, generators)

4. The electromagnet in an electric motor keeps changing _____.
   (size, direction)

5. Even an electrically run generator needs _____
   to keep working. (an electric motor, like poles)

C. Answer the questions.

1. What is an electric motor? _____

   _____

   _____

2. What do electric motors use? _____

   _____

   _____

3. In an electric motor, what is the north pole of the electromagnet always

   lined up with? _____

   _____

   _____

Electronics

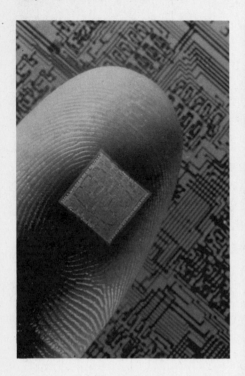

A microchip can have hundreds of transistors and other electronic devices.

Electronics is the branch of science that makes things such as radios, stereos, televisions, calculators, and computers. You have learned about machines that use electricity for energy. But electronic devices use electricity in another way. Electronic devices change electricity into signals. These signals can represent sounds, pictures, and numbers.

Transistors are tiny devices used to change current electricity into signals. Transistors do three main jobs. Some transistors change alternating current into direct current. All electronic devices use direct current. Other transistors make signals stronger. A third kind of transistor changes the signal's frequency.

A regular electric current flows through a conductor. But the current in electronic devices flows through a **semiconductor.** A semiconductor is a kind of matter that is not a very good conductor or insulator. But it can control an electric current. Many electronic devices use the semiconductor **silicon.**

You may have heard of something called a **microchip.** Most microchips are made of silicon. A tiny microchip much smaller than your fingernail can hold enough transistors to run a watch.

Without electronics, our lives would be very different. We could not listen to the radio or stereo. We could not watch television. We would depend on newspapers to know what was happening in the world.

A. Use the words below to complete the sentences.

different	microchips	silicon
direct	semiconductor	transistors
Electronics	signals	

1. _____ is the branch of science that makes things such as radios, televisions, calculators, and computers.

2. Electronic devices change electricity into _____.

3. Electronic devices use _____ to change current electricity into signals.

4. All electronic devices use _____ current.

5. The current in electronic devices flows through a

   _____.

6. Many electronic devices use the semiconductor _____.

B. Answer True or False.

1. Electronic devices use electricity only for energy. _____

2. Electronic devices can change electricity into signals that can

   represent sounds, pictures, or numbers. _____

3. All electronic devices use direct current. _____

4. One kind of transistor makes the signals weaker. _____

5. A semiconductor can control an electric current. _____

C. Answer the question.

What are the three main jobs that transistors do? _____

_____

_____

_____

Using Electricity Safely

Cover an outlet when it is not being used.

Machines run by electricity make life easier. But any machine or tool run by electricity must be used safely. Electricity can be dangerous.

People should take care when using electric outlets. Outlets are meant for plugging in electric cords only. Never put anything else into an electric outlet. An object put into an outlet can carry electricity. Electricity can burn the hand of the person holding the object. When cleaning or fixing an appliance, be sure to pull the plug out of the outlet. An appliance that is still plugged in can give a bad shock.

Water is a good conductor of electricity. Keep electric appliances away from water. For example, never wash or bathe with a hair dryer near you. If the appliance fell into the water, the electric shock could kill you instantly.

Answer the questions.

1. Why should you not keep a radio near a person bathing? _____

   _____

   _____

2. Why should you never put anything other than a plug into an outlet? _____

   _____

■ Review

Part A

Fill in the missing words.

1. Magnetism is a pulling force that certain metals, called

   _____ , have. (compasses, magnets)

2. If an iron bar is placed inside a coil of wire when electricity flows

   through it, an _____ is formed.
   (electric generator, electromagnet)

3. Electronic devices change electricity into _____. (signals, volts)

4. The path taken by an electric current is called

   _____. (a volt, an electric circuit)

5. An electric motor is a machine that changes electric energy into

   _____ energy. (chemical, mechanical)

6. Dry cells and batteries store _____.
   (magnetism, electricity)

7. To keep fires from starting, _____ are put in circuits. (volts, fuses)

Part B

Read each sentence. Write <u>True</u> if the sentence is true. Write <u>False</u> if the sentence is false.

1. A volt measures the amount of push a source of electricity gives the

   electricity. _____

2. The north pole of one magnet attracts the north pole of another

   magnet. _____

3. A battery is two or more dry cells working together. _____

4. A kind of matter that electrons can move through easily is an

   insulator. _____

5. Electric motors use electromagnets and regular magnets. _____

Fill in the circle in front of the word or phrase that best completes the sentences. The first one is done for you.

1. A dry cell has two posts called
   - ● terminals.
   - ⓑ circuits.
   - ⓒ batteries.

2. The measure of the push a source of electricity has is
   - ⓐ electrons.
   - ⓑ a shock.
   - ⓒ volts.

3. Generators get electricity by
   - ⓐ circuit breakers.
   - ⓑ electric outlets.
   - ⓒ electromagnetic induction.

4. The attracting area around every magnet is
   - ⓐ electricity.
   - ⓑ a magnetic field.
   - ⓒ a terminal.

5. Electric motors change electric energy into
   - ⓐ mechanical energy.
   - ⓑ magnetism.
   - ⓒ chemical energy.

6. Short circuits can
   - ⓐ make a closed circuit.
   - ⓑ start fires.
   - ⓒ make an open circuit.

7. Tons of iron can be lifted by
   - ⓐ north and south poles.
   - ⓑ fuses.
   - ⓒ electromagnets.

8. People should take care when using
   - ⓐ electric outlets.
   - ⓑ magnetism.
   - ⓒ compasses.

9. The electric current in electronic devices flows through
   - ⓐ a semiconductor.
   - ⓑ a conductor.
   - ⓒ an insulator.

10. Alternating current
    - ⓐ moves in the same direction all the time.
    - ⓑ is made by batteries.
    - ⓒ happens when the electron flow changes directions.

Just for Fun

Use the clues to solve the puzzle. Use the words below.

another	electricity	lift	rid
atom	good	magnetism	safely
charged	iron	one	terminals
compasses			

Across

1. The north pole of one magnet attracts the south pole of _____ magnet.
4. An electromagnet can _____ tons of iron.
6. When electrons leave their atoms, matter becomes electrically _____.
7. The force that magnets have is _____.
9. As long as an _____ has the same number of protons and electrons, the atom has no charge.
10. An electromagnet has an _____ bar inside a coil of wire.
12. It is important to use electricity _____.

Down

2. The electric outlets in your house provide alternating current _____.
3. An atom that loses, or gets _____ of electrons, has a positive charge.
5. A dry cell has two posts called _____.
6. Sailors use _____ to tell which direction they are going.
8. Rubber is a _____ insulator.
11. A magnet has a north pole at _____ end and a south pole at the other end.

What Is Motion?

1

2

Has this car moved?

3

4

Has this car moved?

Suppose you are looking out a window. You see a car going by. The car is in **motion**. In motion means moving. But how do you really know the car is in motion?

Look at pictures 1 and 2 on this page. In picture 1, the car is to the right of the tree. In picture 2, after 2 seconds, the car is to the left of the tree. The tree cannot move from one place to another. So the car must have moved from one place to another. The car must have been in motion.

Now look at pictures 3 and 4. Picture 3 and picture 4 are 2 seconds apart. Did the car move? You cannot tell. You cannot tell whether an object is in motion unless you have a **frame of reference.** A frame of reference is some other object to which you compare an object's position. In this case, you have no frame of reference. So you cannot tell whether the car is in motion. An object is in motion only in relation to other objects.

Have you ever ridden on an airplane at night? If you have, you know that you do not feel like the plane is moving. Unless you can see lights from the window, you have no frame of reference. You know the plane is in motion in relation to Earth. But you feel as though the plane were still.

Scientists always use a frame of reference to talk about motion. For example, when they study the motion of stars in the sky, they use other stars as a frame of reference. Only in this way can they know the stars are moving.

A. Answer True or False.

1. In motion means moving. _____

2. Scientists do not use a frame of reference to talk about motion.

   _____

3. You cannot tell whether an object is in motion unless you have a frame of reference. _____

4. A frame of reference is some other object to which you compare an object's position. _____

5. When scientists study the motion of stars in the sky, they use clouds as a frame of reference. _____

B. Answer the questions.

1   2   3

1. Look at picture 1 and then at picture 2, which was taken later. Is the train in motion? _____

2. How do you know? _____

   _____

3. Which is the frame of reference, the train or the countryside? ____

   _____

4. In picture 3, can you tell if train A is in motion? _____

5. In picture 3, can you tell if train B is in motion? _____

6. Explain your answers to questions 4 and 5. _____

   _____

If the direction of motion changes, velocity changes.

If the speed of motion changes, velocity also changes.

You know a car is in motion if you see it in one place and then in another place, in relation to an object. Motion can change in several ways.

One thing that can change about motion is its **speed.** Speed is the distance something moves in a certain time. Many people can walk 2 miles in 1 hour. Their speed is 2 miles per hour. It is written 2 miles/hour. Some people can run 7 miles an hour, or 7 miles/hour. The speed of 7 miles/hour is faster than 2 miles/hour.

Another thing that can change about motion is its **velocity.** Velocity is speed in a certain direction. If you are running at 7 miles/hour along a straight path, your velocity is the same as your speed. But if you are running around a track, you are changing your direction. So your speed is the same, but your velocity is changing. Velocity changes when the direction of the motion changes.

You can also change your velocity by changing your speed. This change in velocity is called **acceleration.** If you pedal a bicycle so that it speeds up, that is positive acceleration. If you use the brakes to slow down, that is negative acceleration.

A. Use the words below to complete the sentences.

acceleration	negative	speed
motion	positive	velocity

1. The distance something moves in a certain time is _____.

2. Speed in a certain direction is _____.

3. A change in velocity is _____.

4. If motion speeds up, it is _____ acceleration.

5. If motion slows down, it is _____ acceleration.

B. Underline the correct words.

1. You know a car is (accelerating, in motion) if you see it in one place and then in another place.

2. You can change your velocity by changing your (speed, distance).

3. Motion can change in (one way, several ways).

4. If you use brakes on a bicycle to slow down, that is negative (acceleration, velocity).

C. Answer the questions.

1. What is the difference between positive and negative acceleration?

_____

_____

2. What is speed? _____

_____

3. In what two ways can velocity be changed? _____

_____

Balanced and Unbalanced Forces

Suppose your teacher asked you to move a heavy desk in your classroom. How would you move it? You might get on one side of the desk and start pushing. Or you might grab the legs and start pulling. Either way, you would be using a **force.** Any push or pull is a force.

The force you use in pushing or pulling the desk has a size. You could use a small amount of force or a lot of force. Forces differ in size. Another way forces differ is in direction. A force can be left or right, or up or down.

The desk will not move by itself. A force is needed to put the desk in motion. But even when the desk is not moving, forces are acting on it. The floor is actually pushing up on the desk. At the same time, the force of gravity is pulling down on it. If the desk is not in motion, the upward push is the same as the downward pull. The size of the forces is the same, but the directions of the forces are different. Whenever forces are the same in size but opposite in direction, they are balanced forces. An object that is not in motion will never move if balanced forces act on it.

How can you move the desk? You can move it because you unbalance the forces. The size of your force is greater than the force of air pushing on the other side of the desk. Unbalanced forces act in opposite directions but differ in size. If unbalanced forces act on an object, the object will always move in the direction of the greater force.

A. Answer True or False.

1. Any push or pull is a force. _____

2. Forces do not differ in direction. _____

3. A force is needed to put things in motion. _____

4. When an object is not moving, forces are not acting on it.

   _____

5. Forces different in size but the same in direction are balanced

   forces. _____

6. Unbalanced forces act in opposite directions but differ in size.

   _____

B. Answer the questions.

1. Why does a heavy desk not move by itself? _____

   _____

2. When a heavy desk is not moving, what kind of forces are acting

   on it? _____

   _____

3. If unbalanced forces act on a desk, the desk will always move in

   which direction? _____

   _____

C. Write the letter for the correct answer.

1. An object that is not in motion will _____ move if balanced
   forces act on it.
   (a) always   (b) sometimes   (c) never

2. You can move an object because you _____ .
   (a) balance gravity   (b) balance forces   (c) unbalance forces

3. Forces differ in _____ .
   (a) size only   (b) direction only   (c) size and direction

101

Gravity

The same force of gravity makes dead leaves fall to the ground and keeps the moon moving in a circle around Earth.

Gravity is a force that attracts, or pulls on, matter. On Earth, gravity attracts all matter to the ground. Leaves from a tree, raindrops, or a ball you throw in the air are all pulled to the ground by Earth's force of gravity.

Earth is not the only object that has gravity. All matter has gravity. The more mass matter has, the greater the force of its gravity. Earth has a great amount of mass. So the gravity of Earth itself is stronger than the gravity of anything on Earth. It is the pull of Earth's gravity that gives weight to all matter on Earth. How much you weigh is the amount of pull on the mass of your body.

The moon has gravity. Since the moon has less mass than Earth, it has less gravity. The moon's gravity is about one sixth as strong as Earth's. Why doesn't the motion of the moon make the moon fly off into space? The greater force of Earth's gravity pulls the moon. So instead of flying off into space or being pulled to Earth, the moon keeps moving in a circle around Earth.

All the other planets have gravity, too. So does the sun. Since the sun's gravity is the strongest, it pulls on all the planets. The planets keep moving in a circle around the sun.

A. Fill in the missing words.

1. Gravity is a force that _____ matter. (attracts, repels)

2. On Earth, gravity attracts all matter to the _____ . (sky, ground)

3. The more mass matter has, the _____ the force of its gravity. (less, greater)

4. Earth's gravity gives _____ to matter. (weight, mass)

5. The moon _____ gravity. (has, does not have)

B. Mark with an __X__ each happening that is caused by gravity.

1. A bulb in a lamp lights up. _____

2. You weigh more than a baby. _____

3. The moon moves in a circle around Earth. _____

4. Birds sing. _____

5. A ball thrown in the air falls to the ground. _____

C. Use each word to write a sentence about gravity.

1. force _____

_____

2. weight _____

_____

3. planets _____

_____

D. Answer the question.

Why does the moon have less gravity than Earth? _____

_____

_____

If forces are balanced, an object at rest will stay at rest until . . .

the forces become unbalanced.

About 300 years ago, a scientist named Isaac Newton had some ideas about forces and motion. His ideas became known as Newton's laws of motion. They are called laws because they correctly explain certain happenings around you.

One of Newton's laws says that if all the forces acting on an object are balanced, the object will keep its state of motion. In other words, if the object is at rest, or not moving, it will stay at rest. If the object is moving, it will keep on moving. The state of motion will stay the same unless the forces become unbalanced by some other force.

Suppose you see a soccer ball on the grass. It is at rest. The force of the ground pushing up on it is balanced by the force of gravity pulling down on it. The soccer ball will keep its state of motion, which in this case is no motion. Suppose you kick the ball. You have unbalanced the forces with the force of your kick. The ball will be in motion. The ball will stay in motion until some other force comes along. In this case, a force called friction will stop the ball after a while.

Another law of motion says that for every action there is an equal and opposite reaction. When a rocket is launched, burning fuel makes hot gases come out of the bottom of the rocket. The gases push down against Earth. The rocket takes off, moving away from Earth. The gases pushing down is the action. The rocket moving up is the reaction.

A. Use the words below to complete the sentences.

action	gravity	reaction
balanced	laws	unbalanced

1. Isaac Newton's ideas about forces and motion became known as Newton's _____ of motion.

2. If all the forces acting on an object are _____, the object will keep its state of motion.

3. The state of motion will stay the same until the forces become _____ by some other force.

4. The force of the ground pushing up on an object at rest is balanced by the force of _____ pulling down on it.

5. For every action, there is an equal and opposite _____.

B. Write the word or words that best finish each sentence.

1. If an object is at rest, it will stay at _____.

2. If an object is moving, it will continue _____.

3. For every _____, there is an equal and opposite reaction.

C. Answer True or False.

1. An object will keep its state of motion if the forces acting on it are unbalanced. _____

2. The law of action and reaction explains how a rocket takes off from Earth. _____

3. If you kick a soccer ball that is at rest, you have balanced the forces acting on it. _____

4. Friction will stop a moving ball after a while. _____

Space Travel

A Weather Satellite

Scientists use what they know about forces and motion when they send rockets into space. Gravity pulls things toward Earth. In order to lift rockets into space, powerful engines are needed. The force of the rocket engines must be greater than the force of gravity. In that way the rockets can escape Earth's powerful pull.

Some rockets carry **satellites.** Once a satellite is in space, the force from its engine balances the force from Earth's gravity. Then the satellite circles Earth the way the moon circles Earth. Some satellites are put into space to study the weather on Earth. Other satellites send radio and television signals around the world. Some rockets explore other planets and their natural satellites, or moons.

A. **Answer the questions.**

1. What do scientists need to know about to send rockets into space?

   _____

   _____

   _____

2. What are needed to lift rockets into space? _____

   _____

   _____

B. **Answer <u>True</u> or <u>False</u>.**

1. Rockets do not carry satellites. _____

2. Some satellites study weather on Earth. _____

3. Some rockets explore other planets. _____

Review

Part A

Write the letter for the correct answer.

1. You cannot tell whether there is motion unless you have a _____.
   (a) picture   (b) frame of reference   (c) window

2. Speed is the distance something moves in a certain _____.
   (a) direction   (b) velocity   (c) time

3. Velocity is speed in a certain _____.
   (a) direction   (b) distance   (c) time

4. Any push or pull is _____.
   (a) gravity   (b) a force   (c) matter

5. Forces differ in size and _____.
   (a) speed   (b) distance   (c) direction

6. Gravity is a force that attracts _____.
   (a) matter   (b) energy   (c) weight

7. If forces acting on an object are balanced, the object will keep its state

   of _____.
   (a) motion   (b) gravity   (c) matter

8. For every action, there is an equal and opposite _____.
   (a) direction   (b) weight   (c) reaction

Part B

Read each sentence. Write True if the sentence is true. Write False if the sentence is false.

1. A change in velocity is called acceleration. _____

2. Whenever forces are the same in size but opposite in direction, they

   are balanced forces. _____

3. An object is in motion only in relation to other objects. _____

4. A force is never needed to put things in motion. _____

5. Earth's gravity gives weight to all matter on Earth. _____

UNIT 6 ▪ Test

Fill in the circle in front of the word or phrase that best completes the sentences. The first one is done for you.

1. For every action, there is an equal and opposite
   - ● reaction.
   - ⓑ velocity.
   - ⓒ frame of reference.

2. Isaac Newton's ideas became known as the laws of
   - ⓐ speed.
   - ⓑ motion.
   - ⓒ acceleration.

3. Gravity is
   - ⓐ motion.
   - ⓑ a force.
   - ⓒ matter.

4. Any push or pull is
   - ⓐ motion.
   - ⓑ gravity.
   - ⓒ a force.

5. Unbalanced forces act in opposite directions but differ in
   - ⓐ size.
   - ⓑ distance.
   - ⓒ time.

6. The pull of Earth's gravity gives things
   - ⓐ motion.
   - ⓑ weight.
   - ⓒ mass.

7. If you pedal a bicycle so it speeds up, that is
   - ⓐ velocity.
   - ⓑ positive acceleration.
   - ⓒ negative acceleration.

8. Motion depends on
   - ⓐ a frame of reference.
   - ⓑ speed.
   - ⓒ a reaction.

9. An object at rest
   - ⓐ will stay at rest.
   - ⓑ will start moving.
   - ⓒ is unbalanced.

10. The more mass some matter has, the greater the force of its
    - ⓐ frame of reference.
    - ⓑ motion.
    - ⓒ gravity.

Each sentence below is about motion and forces. But one word in each sentence is scrambled. Unscramble the letters. Then write the correct word on the spaces at the right. Choose from the words below. The first one is done for you.

differ	lift	speeds
force	motion	time
gravity	never	velocity

1. Any push or pull is a COFER.

   ___ ___ ___ ___ ___
   1   15

2. YETCOVIL is speed in a certain direction.

   ___ ___ ___ ___ ___ ___ ___ ___
       9   6

3. Speed is the distance something moves in a certain MITE.

   ___ ___ ___ ___
   4 11

4. Forces FIDREF in size and direction.

   ___ ___ ___ ___ ___ ___
       10   13 2

5. Powerful engines are needed to FLIT rockets into space.

   ___ ___ ___ ___
       7

6. VAYTRIG attracts matter.

   ___ ___ ___ ___ ___ ___ ___
       8 3

7. An object at rest will VEREN move if balanced forces act on it.

   ___ ___ ___ ___ ___
   14   12

8. It is positive acceleration if a car DESEPS up.

   ___ ___ ___ ___ ___ ___
             16 5

Solve the Secret Message. When a letter of a word above has a number under it, write that letter above the same number in the Secret Message.

Secret Message: To tell if something is in motion, you need a

___ ___ ___ ___ ___   ___ ___   ___ ___ ___ ___ ___ ___ ___ ___ ___ .
1 2 3 4 5   6 7   8 9 10 11 12 13 14 15 16

UNIT 7 · Machines

What Is Work?

This box is being moved. Is work being done?

You probably do many kinds of work. You may do work for school. You may do work around your house, such as mowing the lawn. You may work at a job. But these things are not what scientists call work. For scientists, work has a special meaning.

For scientists, **work** is the use of force to move an object. In order for an action to be work, the force used must be in the same direction as the motion.

If you pushed as hard as you could against a heavy desk and the desk did not move, you would not be doing work. Work only happens when an object moves.

Lifting a box is work. When you lift a box, you use a force to move the box. You pull upward on the box, and the box moves upward.

But carrying a box is not work. When you carry a box, you are using force to keep the box from falling. The force is an upward force. But the box is moving forward as you walk. The force and the motion are not in the same direction. So no work is being done.

In this unit you will learn more about work and how people make work easier to do.

A. Use the words below to complete the sentences.

direction	force	work

1. For scientists, _____ has a special meaning.

2. Work is the use of _____ to move an object.

3. In order for an action to be work, the force used must be in the same _____ as the motion.

B. Answer <u>True</u> or <u>False</u>.

1. Scientists would call watching TV work. _____

2. If you pushed as hard as you could against a heavy desk, and the desk didn't move, you would be doing work. _____

3. Work only happens when an object moves. _____

4. Lifting a box is not work. _____

5. Carrying a box is not work because the force and the motion are not in the same direction. _____

6. When you lift a box, you pull upward on the box, and the box moves downward. _____

C. Use each word to write a sentence about work.

1. force _____

_____

2. motion _____

_____

3. direction _____

_____

Friction

Friction is the rubbing of one object against another. It is a force that resists, or works against, motion. It slows down moving objects. Every motion that takes place on Earth is affected by friction. Without friction, life would be very different.

You could not walk without friction to keep your feet from sliding on the ground. Concrete, grass, and dirt are rough surfaces. Rough surfaces provide more friction than smooth surfaces. If you have ever tried to walk on ice, you know that your feet slip and slide. Smooth surfaces such as ice provide very little friction.

Without friction, you could not pick things up and hold them. Everything you tried to hold would slip through your hands and fall.

Without friction, cars could not move. Their tires would not hold on to the road. When a car gets stuck in mud, the wheels turn around, but the car does not move. Mud does not provide enough friction for the tires to hold.

Have you ever tried to push a heavy box? Friction between the ground and the box makes this difficult. You can make the box easier to push by taking some things out of the box. This makes the box lighter. The heavier something is, the more friction slows it down.

Friction makes heat. Try rubbing your hands together. You will feel them getting warmer. When you rub two sticks together, they get warmer and warmer. When they get hot enough, they start to burn.

Friction keeps you from slipping.

A. Use the words below to complete the sentences.

friction	little	resists
heat	motion	

1. The rubbing of one object against another is _____.

2. Friction is a force that _____, or works against, motion.

3. Every _____ that takes place on Earth is affected by friction.

4. Smooth surfaces such as ice provide very _____ friction.

5. Friction makes _____.

B. Underline the correct words.

1. Friction keeps your feet from (walking, sliding) on the ground.

2. The heavier something is, the more friction (slows it down, speeds it up).

3. If you rub your hands together, you will feel them getting (warm, cold).

4. Without friction, life would be (the same, very different).

5. Friction makes it (difficult, easy) to push heavy objects along the ground.

C. For motions which friction helps, write **H**. For motions which friction makes difficult, write **D**.

1. pushing a heavy box _____

2. picking things up _____

3. walking _____

4. driving a car _____

5. making a fire _____

What Are Machines?

A wagon and a car are two machines that make work easier.

It is easier to pull a large rock in a wagon than to push it on the ground. It is easier to tighten a nut with a wrench than with your fingers. It is easier to raise a car with a jack than to lift it yourself. A wagon, a wrench, and a jack are all machines. Machines make work easier.

Some machines cut down on friction. Others can change the amount of force used. Still others can change the direction of the force used. Some machines do more than one of these things.

It is easier to pull a large rock in a wagon because the wagon's wheels cut down on friction. When the rock is on the ground, all of the rock that is touching the ground provides friction. When the rock is in the wagon, only the wheels touch the ground. The wheels use the friction with the ground to turn and move the rock.

It is easier to tighten a nut with a wrench because it makes the amount of force larger. A machine that changes the direction of the force is the pulley you use to open curtains. When you pull down on the cord, the curtains open.

If there were no machines, you would have to walk everywhere. There would be no bicycles, cars, trains, buses, or planes. There would be no wagons or wheelbarrows to move things. It is hard to imagine what life would be like without machines.

A. Draw lines to match the machines with the work they can do for you.

1. wrench   raise a car

2. wagon   tighten a nut

3. jack   pull a large rock

B. Fill in the missing words.

1. Machines make work _____. (easier, harder)

2. The wagon's wheels cut down on _____. (speed, friction)

3. A wrench makes the amount of the force _____.
(larger, smaller)

4. A pulley changes the _____ of the force.
(speed, direction)

5. It is _____ to raise a car with a jack than to lift it yourself.
(easier, harder)

C. List three ways machines make work easier.

1. _____

_____

2. _____

_____

3. _____

_____

D. Use each word in a sentence about machines.

1. force _____

_____

2. friction _____

_____

Lever

Inclined Plane

Wedge

Screw

Pulley

Wheel and Axle

There are thousands of different kinds of machines. You use machines every day. But did you know that all machines are based on only six kinds of **simple machines?** The six simple machines are the **lever, inclined plane, wedge, screw, pulley,** and **wheel and axle.** Look at their pictures on this page.

A lever is a rod that can turn on a point called a **fulcrum.** If you push down on the end of one kind of lever, the other end moves up. You can lift things more easily because less force is needed. There are three basic kinds of levers. They are different because each kind has the fulcrum in a different place.

An inclined plane is a flat surface that slopes. A board from a low place to a high place is an inclined plane called a ramp. Less force is needed to slide an object up a ramp than to lift the object.

A wedge is two inclined planes that come together in a point. You can split a log more easily by hitting a wedge stuck in the log than by hitting the log with an ax. A screw is an inclined plane wrapped around a rod. Screws hold things together better than nails.

A pulley is a wheel with a rope around it. You can fasten an object to one end of the rope. If you pull the other end, you can lift the object. Several pulleys can be joined together to make it easy to lift heavy objects. A wheel and axle is really a kind of lever that continues to turn around its fulcrum.

A. Use the words below to label each machine.

| inclined plane | pulley | wedge |
| lever | screw | wheel and axle |

1. _____

4. _____

2. _____

5. _____

3. _____

6. _____

B. Answer <u>True</u> or <u>False</u>.

1. There are 12 kinds of simple machines. _____

2. A fulcrum is the point that a lever turns on. _____

3. Pulleys cannot be joined together. _____

4. Screws hold things together better than nails. _____

5. Less force is needed to slide an object up a ramp than to lift the object. _____

A compound machine is made of two or more simple machines.

Try pulling a nail out of wood with your fingers. It is very hard to do. But with the end of a claw hammer, it is easy to get the nail out. The hammer is a lever. It increases the force you put on the nail.

Compound machines can make work even easier than simple machines. A compound machine is a simple machine connected to one or more other simple machines. In a compound machine, the force you pass on to one simple machine is made larger and passed on to another simple machine. In this way, the total force is made much larger.

Compound machines are all around you. A scissors is a compound machine. It is simply two levers, with the fulcrum where the pin is. A can opener is a compound machine. The two handles are levers. The key you turn to open a can is a wheel and axle. The blade that cuts into the can is a wedge. A bicycle is another compound machine. Its wheels are connected to axles. So they make a wheel-and-axle machine. The brake handles are levers.

A machine cannot make energy. But every machine needs energy. When you pedal a bicycle, you provide the energy. Many machines use electric energy.

All machines waste energy. Remember that friction is a force that resists motion. Machines usually have moving parts that rub against each other. Friction slows down the motion of the parts. So energy is wasted. The work done by a machine is always less than the work put into it.

A. Write the letter for the correct answer.

1. A simple machine connected to one or more other simple machines is _____ machine.
   (a) a big　　(b) a compound　　(c) an electric

2. In a compound machine, the total force is _____ .
   (a) made much less　　(b) the same　　(c) made much larger

3. A machine cannot make _____ .
   (a) products　　(b) friction　　(c) energy

4. Every machine needs _____ .
   (a) energy　　(b) friction　　(c) electricity

5. The work done by a machine is always _____ the work put into it.
   (a) less than　　(b) the same as　　(c) more than

B. Answer True or False.

1. When you pedal a bicycle, you provide the energy. _____

2. Friction speeds up the motion of the parts of a machine. _____

3. In a compound machine, the force put on one simple machine is made larger and put on another simple machine. _____

4. All machines waste energy. _____ .

5. Machines usually have moving parts that rub against each other. _____

6. A scissors is a simple machine. _____

7. Many machines use electric energy. _____

C. Use each word to write a sentence about compound machines.

1. simple _____

   _____

2. friction _____

   _____

Gasoline Engines

The Model T was a popular car about 80 years ago.

Gasoline Engine

A car is a compound machine. It is made up of many simple machines. One of the most important parts of a car is its **engine.** The engine is a compound machine, too. In most cars, the engine gets its energy from gasoline. Gasoline is a fuel. Engines that use gasoline as their fuel are called gasoline engines.

A gasoline engine has up to eight tubes called cylinders. The engine also has a carburetor where gasoline is mixed with air. The carburetor sends this mixture to the cylinders. Some gasoline engines do not have carburetors. Instead, a fuel-injection system squirts fuel into the cylinders.

Each cylinder has its own spark plug. When the mixture of gasoline and air reaches the tops of the cylinders, the spark plugs start little fires. The gases from the fires push on pistons inside the cylinders. The pistons move up and down.

The up-and-down motion of the pistons moves another part of the engine called the crankshaft. The motion of the crankshaft gives the energy the car needs for the wheels to turn and for the car to move.

Gasoline engines are not only used in cars. They can also be used in lawn mowers, small boats, trucks, and propeller airplanes.

A. The steps below describe how a gasoline engine makes a car move. Number the steps in the correct order. The first one is done for you.

_____ The spark plugs start little fires.

_____ The motion of the crankshaft makes the car move.

____1____ Gasoline mixes with air in the carburetor.

_____ The motion of the pistons moves the crankshaft.

_____ The mixture of gasoline and air reaches the tops of the cylinders.

_____ Gases from the fires push on pistons inside cylinders.

B. Fill in the missing words.

1. A car is a _____ machine. (compound, simple)

2. The engine of a car is a _____ machine. (compound, simple)

3. In most cars, the engine gets its energy from _____. (air, gasoline)

4. Engines that use gasoline as their fuel are called _____. (compound machines, gasoline engines)

5. Gasoline engines are _____ used in cars. (only, not only)

C. Draw lines to complete the sentences.

1. Pistons   has its own spark plug.

2. Each cylinder   start little fires.

3. A gasoline engine   is a fuel.

4. Spark plugs   move up and down.

5. Gasoline   has up to eight cylinders.

D. Answer the question.

What are five machines that use gasoline engines? _____

_____

Jet Engines

Jet engines make it possible for this jet to fly.

Most large airplanes today are powered by jet engines. Jet engines are compound machines. How do jet engines work?

Air goes into the engine. A compressor squeezes the air, which is then mixed with fuel. The fuel mixture burns and produces hot gases. The gases turn a turbine wheel that runs the compressor. Then the gases rush out of the engine toward the tail of the plane.

Jet engines work because of one of the laws of motion. Remember that for every action there is an equal and opposite reaction. The action is gases rushing out of the engine. The reaction is the motion of the plane in the opposite direction. The gases do not need any matter to push against. Even without air, a jet plane would fly.

Answer <u>True</u> or <u>False</u>.

1. Most large airplanes today are powered by jet engines. _____

2. In a jet plane, hot gases rush out of the engine toward the front of the plane. _____

3. As gases rush out of the plane's engine, the plane moves forward. _____

■ Review

Part A

Underline the correct words.

1. Work only happens when an object (falls, moves).

2. Carrying boxes is not work, because the force and the motion are not (in the same direction, at the same speed).

3. (Work, Friction) is a force that resists motion.

4. Rough surfaces provide (less, more) friction than smooth surfaces.

5. Machines make work (harder, easier).

6. All machines are based on six kinds of (simple, compound) machines.

7. (Less, More) force is needed to slide an object up a ramp than to lift the object.

8. A simple machine connected to one or more other simple machines is (an engine, a compound machine).

9. A machine (can, cannot) make energy.

10. A gasoline engine has up to eight tubes called (carburetors, cylinders).

11. The fuel mixture in a jet plane burns and produces (hot gases, air).

Part B

Read each sentence. Write __True__ if the sentence is true. Write __False__ if the sentence is false.

1. Friction makes heat. _____

2. A wedge is two levers that come together in a point. _____

3. A compound machine is made up of two or more simple machines.

_____

4. Lifting a box is not work. _____

Fill in the circle in front of the word or phrase that best completes the sentences. The first one is done for you.

1. In most cars, the engine gets its energy from
   ⓐ air.
   ● gasoline.
   ⓒ spark plugs.

2. Moving objects are slowed by
   ⓐ work.
   ⓑ friction.
   ⓒ machines.

3. A wheel with a rope around it is
   ⓐ a pulley.
   ⓑ an inclined plane.
   ⓒ a compound machine.

4. Work is made easier by
   ⓐ forces.
   ⓑ motions.
   ⓒ machines.

5. As hot gases leave a jet plane's engine, the plane
   ⓐ moves forward.
   ⓑ moves backward.
   ⓒ stops.

6. All machines are based on only six kinds of
   ⓐ work.
   ⓑ simple machines.
   ⓒ energy.

7. A machine cannot make
   ⓐ energy.
   ⓑ friction.
   ⓒ heat.

8. A lever turns on a
   ⓐ fulcrum.
   ⓑ crankshaft.
   ⓒ turbine.

9. Most cars use
   ⓐ jet engines.
   ⓑ simple machines.
   ⓒ gasoline engines.

10. If a force is used on an object, and the object moves in the same direction as the force, it is
    ⓐ a machine.
    ⓑ an engine.
    ⓒ work.

■ Just for Fun ■

The following sentences are about machines. But one word is missing in each sentence. Write in the missing words on the spaces at the right. Choose from the words below. The first letter of each missing word is written in for you. Read the letters down the first column for a message about machines.

axle	energy	move	resists
car	heat	needs	simple
complex	inclined	out	wedge
down	kind	own	

1. To do work, a force must _____ something.   M _ _ _ _

2. A wheel and _____ is a simple machine.   A _ _ _ _

3. A _____ is a compound machine.   C _ _

4. Friction makes _____.   H _ _ _

5. A ramp is an _____ plane.   I _ _ _ _ _ _ _

6. Every machine _____ energy.   N _ _ _ _

7. A machine cannot make _____.   E _ _ _ _ _

8. There are six kinds of _____ machines.   S _ _ _ _ _

9. Pistons move up and _____.   D _ _ _

10. Hot gases rush _____ of a jet plane's engine.   O _ _

11. A _____ is a simple machine.   W _ _ _ _

12. Each cylinder has its _____ spark plug.   O _ _

13. Friction _____ motion.   R _ _ _ _ _ _

14. Each _____ of lever has a fulcrum.   K _ _ _

125

Computers

Output Device (Screen)

Input Device (Keyboard)

Computer

Computers are machines that can store and work with information. Computers can do math and solve problems. But computers cannot think. People have to give computers specially written instructions. These instructions are called computer **programs.**

There are different kinds of computers. But all computers have some things that are the same. All computers have an **input device,** an **output device,** and a **central processing unit** (CPU).

The input device is used to enter information into the computer. The input device used most often is a keyboard. A computer keyboard is like a typewriter keyboard. Information is put into the computer by typing on the keyboard. The computer translates the typed information and uses it to perform tasks and solve problems.

The output device gives you the information you need from the computer. Most computers have a screen as an output device. The screen is like a TV screen. Most computers also have a printer that prints information from the screen on paper.

The CPU is the part of the computer that stores and works with information. An important part of the CPU is the memory. A computer's memory is like a storeroom for information.

A. **Write the letter for the correct answer.**

1. Computers are machines that can store and work with _____ .
   (a) information   (b) objects   (c) light

2. Computers cannot _____ .
   (a) think   (b) do math   (c) store information

3. The instructions people give computers are _____ .
   (a) output   (b) sounds   (c) programs

4. The input device used most often is a _____ .
   (a) screen   (b) keyboard   (c) television

5. Most computers have a _____ as an output device.
   (a) screen   (b) keyboard   (c) radio

6. An important part of the CPU is the _____ .
   (a) screen   (b) keyboard   (c) memory

B. **Answer True or False.**

1. Computers are machines that can store and work with information. _____

2. Computers can do math and solve problems. _____

3. Computers can think. _____

4. People have to give computers instructions. _____

5. The different kinds of computers don't have anything that is the same. _____

6. A computer keyboard is like a typewriter keyboard. _____

7. The CPU is like a TV screen. _____

C. **Draw lines to match each computer part with the job it does.**

1. input device   gives you information from the computer

2. output device   used to enter information into the computer

3. CPU   stores and works with information

127

Lasers

Laser Light

In Unit 4, you learned that sunlight is made of different colors. The colors are made by light waves of different wavelengths. These light waves are able to travel in different directions.

A **laser** is a machine that makes light that is different from natural light. Laser light has waves of only one wavelength. The waves all travel in the same direction. The crests and troughs of the waves are all lined up with one another. Laser light is much stronger than natural light. Instead of spreading out, it travels in a narrow beam.

Lasers can be used in many ways. Some lasers can cut hard objects. Lasers can even cut diamonds. They cut very evenly and cleanly.

When a laser is focused on an object, the place the laser hits gets very hot. The strong heat of laser light can actually cut through steel. Laser light is also easy to direct and use in very small places. So, lasers are used to weld tiny parts in machines. Doctors also use lasers in surgery. Laser light can burn away diseased body tissue without harming the healthy tissue around it.

Television signals and telephone calls can be sent on laser light. Lasers can carry more signals at once than radio waves. Signals sent on laser light lose very little of their strength.

A. Underline the correct words.

1. A laser is a machine that makes light that is (the same as, different from) natural light.

2. Laser light has waves of (one wavelength, many wavelengths).

3. The waves of laser light all travel in (the same direction, different directions).

4. Laser light is (much weaker, much stronger) than natural light.

5. When a laser is focused on an object, the place the laser hits gets (very hot, very cold).

6. Lasers can carry (more signals, fewer signals) at once than radio waves.

7. Signals sent on laser light lose (most, very little) of their strength.

B. Use the words below to complete the sentences.

burn	cut	travel

1. Some lasers can _____ hard objects.

2. Laser light can _____ away diseased body tissue.

3. The light waves in laser light _____ in a narrow beam.

C. Answer True or False.

1. The crests and troughs of laser light rays are all lined up with one another. _____

2. Instead of traveling in a narrow beam, laser light spreads out. _____

3. Laser light cannot cut diamonds. _____

4. Lasers cut very evenly and cleanly. _____

5. Doctors use lasers in surgery. _____

129

Robots

Robots can do many kinds of jobs.

A **robot** is a machine that can do tasks by itself. Most robots have computers inside them. Information is input into the computer inside a robot. This information tells the robot what to do. Today, robots can be programmed to do jobs that people once had to do.

Many robots are used in factories to work on assembly lines. An assembly line is a place where parts of machines are put together. On an assembly line, workers stand on both sides of a moving belt. Parts for machines are placed on the belt. Workers put together the parts as the belt moves by.

Working on an assembly line is boring work for people. Each worker on an assembly line does one small job, over and over again. Robots can do this work without getting tired or bored.

Robots are also used to do jobs that are dangerous for people. Before robots were invented, people had to paint cars. Breathing paint is very bad for people. Now robots paint cars.

Robots can do many kinds of jobs. They can go where people cannot. Robots can explore deep under the oceans. They can explore outer space and send us new information about other planets.

Some robots have even been programmed to speak. These robots almost seem to be alive. But they are only machines. Robots are not human. They cannot think or do things they are not programmed to do. Robots can only follow the instructions that people give them.

A. Answer True or False.

1. A robot is a machine that can do tasks by itself. _____

2. Robots are never used in factories. _____

3. Most robots have computers inside them. _____

4. Working on an assembly line is fun and interesting work for people. _____

5. Robots can do many kinds of jobs. _____

6. Some robots can think. _____

7. Some robots have been programmed to speak. _____

8. Robots can get tired and bored. _____

9. Robots can explore deep under the oceans. _____

B. Fill in the missing words.

1. Robots are used to do jobs that are _____ for people. (dangerous, fun)

2. Many robots are used in _____ to work on assembly lines. (offices, factories)

3. On an assembly line, workers stand on both sides of a _____. (moving belt, robot)

4. Each worker on an assembly line does _____. (many different jobs, one small job)

5. A _____ is a machine that can do tasks by itself. (television, robot)

C. Use each word to write a sentence about robots.

1. factories _____

_____

2. computers _____

_____

Communications

Communications Satellite

Communication is the sending and receiving of information. Whenever you talk to someone, you are communicating. Whenever you write a letter, or send a picture to a friend, you are communicating. Today, people can communicate with others all over the world.

Technology makes modern communications possible. Technology is the use of science to develop new machines. Today, people use telephones, radio, television, computers, and fax machines to communicate. Fax machines are used for sending printed information or photos over a long distance. Computers can share information with other computers in different places.

Communications satellites send signals long distances. A satellite is an object that orbits, or moves around, Earth. The moon is a natural satellite. Communications satellites are made by people and sent into space. Signals are sent to a satellite. The satellite makes the signals stronger. Then it sends them to other satellites or to a different place on Earth.

Without satellites, we could still use telephones, radio, television, and computers to communicate. But it would be much more difficult to send signals long distances.

A. Use the words below to complete the sentences.

communicating	photos	share
information	satellites	signals

1. Communication is the sending and receiving of _____.

2. Whenever you talk to someone, you are _____.

3. Communications _____ send signals long distances.

4. Fax machines are used for sending printed information or _____ over a long distance.

5. Computers can _____ information with other computers in different places.

6. A satellite makes _____ stronger.

B. Answer **True** or **False**.

1. Today people can communicate with others all over the world. _____

2. Computers cannot share information with other computers in different places. _____

3. A satellite is an object that orbits Earth. _____

4. A satellite makes the signals sent to it weaker. _____

5. Without satellites, we could not use telephones, radios, television, and computers to communicate. _____

6. Without satellites, it would be much more difficult to send signals long distances. _____

C. List five machines that are used for communication. _____
_____

Superconductors

Scientists use superconducting magnets in experiments.

You have learned that a conductor is a kind of matter that electricity moves through easily. But when electricity moves through a conductor, it loses some of its energy because of resistance. Resistance changes some of the electricity into heat energy.

Scientists have discovered that some materials lose their resistance when they get cold. But these materials must be more than 400 degrees below zero. There are other materials that lose their resistance at higher temperatures. Materials that do not resist the flow of electricity are called **superconductors.**

If scientists can learn how to use superconductors in place of regular conductors, electricity can be saved. No electricity would be lost between the power plant and the place where it is used.

Underline the correct words.

1. When electricity moves through a conductor, it loses some of its energy because of (gravity, resistance).

2. Resistance changes some electricity into (heat energy, water).

3. Materials that do not resist the flow of electricity are called (conductors, superconductors).

■ Review

Part A

Underline the correct words.

1. (Telephones, Computers) are machines that can store and work with information.

2. Some materials lose their resistance when they get very (cold, hot).

3. Television signals and telephone calls can be sent (through water, on laser light).

4. (Robots, Laser light) can be programmed to do jobs that people once had to do.

5. Most robots have (fax machines, computers) inside them.

6. Whenever you talk to someone, you are (communicating, conducting).

7. Without (typewriters, satellites) it would be much more difficult to send signals long distances.

Part B

Read each sentence. Write <u>True</u> if the sentence is true. Write <u>False</u> if the sentence is false.

1. The output device is used to enter information into a computer. _____

2. Laser light is much stronger than natural light. _____

3. Lasers can carry fewer signals at once than radio waves. _____

4. The CPU is the part of the computer that stores and works with information. _____

5. Robots can do work without getting tired or bored. _____

6. Fax machines are used for sending music. _____

7. A conductor is a kind of matter that electricity cannot move through.

_____

Fill in the circle in front of the word or phrase that best completes the sentences. The first one is done for you.

1. Computers are machines that can store and work with
   - ● information.
   - ⓑ electricity.
   - ⓒ superconductors.

2. An important part of the CPU is the
   - ⓐ input device.
   - ⓑ memory.
   - ⓒ output device.

3. Today people can communicate with others
   - ⓐ only in their city.
   - ⓑ only in their state.
   - ⓒ all over the world.

4. Robots can do
   - ⓐ one job.
   - ⓑ many kinds of jobs.
   - ⓒ only a few jobs.

5. Robots are not
   - ⓐ human.
   - ⓑ useful.
   - ⓒ machines.

6. Laser light has waves of
   - ⓐ many wavelengths.
   - ⓑ two wavelengths.
   - ⓒ only one wavelength.

7. Lasers can send
   - ⓐ letters.
   - ⓑ signals.
   - ⓒ packages.

8. Communications satellites receive signals and
   - ⓐ make them stronger.
   - ⓑ make them weaker.
   - ⓒ increase their frequency.

9. Resistance works against the flow of
   - ⓐ water.
   - ⓑ photons.
   - ⓒ electricity.

10. Materials that do not resist the flow of electricity are called
    - ⓐ superconductors.
    - ⓑ nonresistors.
    - ⓒ insulators.

Just for Fun

Fill in the missing words in each sentence. Use the words below.

CPU	laser	memory
Earth	light	robot
energy	machine	signal

1. When electricity moves through a conductor, it loses some of its _ _ _ _ _ _ .
   2   9

2. A machine that can do tasks by itself is a _ _ _ _ _ .
                                              6

3. A machine that makes light that is different from natural light is a _ _ _ _ _ .
   7

4. The part of a computer that is like a storeroom for information is its _ _ _ _ _ _ .
                                                                         8   10

5. Communications satellites orbit _ _ _ _ _ .
                                    1

6. The part of a computer that stores and works with information is its _ _ _ .
   3

7. Lasers make a very strong kind of _ _ _ _ _ .
                                      4

8. You can send printed materials on a fax _ _ _ _ _ _ _ .
                                                      5

Solve the Secret Message. When a letter of a word above has a number under it, write that letter above the same number in the Secret Message.

Secret Message: Your life is easier because of

_ _ _ _ _ _ _ _ _ _ .
1 2 3 4 5 6 7 8 9 10

GLOSSARY

acceleration, page 98.

Acceleration is a change in velocity. Speeding up is positive acceleration, and slowing down is negative acceleration.

acid, page 30.

An acid is a compound made of molecules that have a positive electric charge. Acids taste sour and turn blue litmus paper red. Strong acids can dissolve metal.

alkali, page 30.

An alkali is a base that can be dissolved in water.

alternating current, page 76.

Alternating current happens when the electron flow changes directions. The electric outlets in a house provide alternating current electricity.

amperes, page 78.

Electric current is measured in amperes. The number of amperes tells how strong the current is.

amplitude, page 54.

The amplitude of a wave is one half the distance between the wave's crest and its trough.

atom, page 8.

An atom is a tiny piece of matter. Atoms are made of three kinds of particles: protons, neutrons, and electrons.

atomic number, page 16.

The atomic number of an element is the number of protons in the nucleus of one of its atoms. No two elements have the same atomic number.

auditory canal, page 60.

The auditory canal is a tube in the ear. Sound waves move down the auditory canal to the eardrum.

auditory nerves, page 60.

The auditory nerves turn the movements of hairs inside the ear into signals. Then the nerves send the signals to the brain.

base, page 30.

A base is a compound made of molecules that have a negative electric charge. Bases taste bitter, feel soapy, and turn red litmus paper blue.

battery, page 82.

A battery is two or more dry cells working together. A battery is used to start a car's engine.

central processing unit (CPU), page 126.

The central processing unit is the part of a computer that stores and works with information.

chemical change, page 26.

A chemical change happens whenever there is a change in a substance's molecules. In a chemical change, energy causes atoms to break free of their molecules and form new, different molecules.

chemical energy, page 36.

Chemical energy is released when fuels are burned.

chemical reaction, page 28.

A chemical reaction is a chemical change. In chemical reactions, molecules are changed.

circuit, page 78.

An electric circuit is the path taken by an electric current.

circuit breaker, page 80.

A circuit breaker is a kind of switch that works like a fuse. It can break a circuit if the current is too great.

communication, page 132.

Communication is the sending and receiving of information.

compound, page 20.

A compound is a substance that is made from molecules of more than one element. A compound differs from the elements it is made of.

compound machine, page 118.

A compound machine is a simple machine connected to one or more other simple machines. In a compound machine, the force passed on to one simple machine is made larger and passed on to another.

computer, page 126.

A computer is a machine that can store and work with information. All computers have an input device, an output device, and a central processing unit.

concave, page 68.

A concave lens is thinner in the middle than it is at the edges. It bends light rays so that they spread apart.

conduct, page 12.

Metals conduct heat and electricity. That is, they let heat and electricity pass through them.

conduction, page 40.
The way heat passes through solids is called conduction.

conductor, page 76.
A conductor is a kind of matter that electrons can move through easily. Metal wire is a common conductor.

convection, page 40.
Convection is the way heat passes through liquids and gases.

convection current, page 40.
A convection current is the movement of molecules in a liquid or a gas when it is heated.

convex, page 68.
A convex lens is thicker in the middle than it is at the edges. It bends light rays so that they come together.

cornea, page 70.
The cornea is the thin covering of the eyeball. It helps protect the eye.

crest, page 54.
The crest is the highest part of a wave.

current electricity, page 76.
Current electricity is the movement of electrically charged particles in the same direction.

direct current, page 76.
Direct current happens when the electron flow is in the same direction all the time. Batteries produce direct current electricity.

dry cell, page 82.
A dry cell is a container that holds a paste of chemicals. As the chemicals react, a flow of electrons forms a direct electric current.

ductile, page 12.
Ductile materials can be easily shaped into a new form. Metals are ductile.

eardrum, page 60.
The eardrum is a thin piece of skin across the auditory canal. Sound waves make the eardrum vibrate.

electric charge, page 8.
An atom has an electric charge when the number of its electrons is not the same as the number of its protons.

electric energy, page 36.
Electric energy is energy in the form of electricity. It makes light bulbs light up and radios play.

electricity, page 74.
Electricity is caused by matter that has an electric charge.

electromagnet, page 86.
An electromagnet is formed when electricity flows through a coil of wire around an iron bar.

electromagnetic induction, page 86.
When a magnet is moved in and out of a coil of wire, electricity flows through the coil. This way of making electricity is electromagnetic induction.

electron, page 8.
An electron is a particle that moves around the nucleus of an atom. It has a negative electric charge.

electronics, page 90.
Electronics is the branch of science that makes things such as radios, stereos, televisions, calculators, and computers.

element, page 10.
An element is the simplest form of matter. It is made of only one kind of atom and cannot be broken down into different substances.

energy, page 36.
Energy is the ability to do work. There are several kinds of energy: mechanical, heat, electric, and chemical.

engine, page 120.
An engine is a compound machine. Some engines use gasoline as fuel.

eyeball, page 70.
The eyeball is the main part of the eye. It is almost round.

filament, page 66.
A filament is a small piece of wire in a light bulb. When electricity passes through the wire, the wire gets hot and gives off light.

focus, page 68.
To focus means to bring light rays together at a point.

force, page 100.
A force is any push or pull. Forces may differ in size or direction.

frame of reference, page 96.
A frame of reference is some other object to which you compare an object's position.

frequency, page 54.
Frequency is the number of waves that move past one spot in a second.

friction, page 112.
Friction is the force that resists, or works against, motion. It is the rubbing of one object against another.

fulcrum, page 116.
A fulcrum is a point on which a lever can turn.

fuse, page 80.
A fuse is a device that is put in a circuit. If the circuit has too much current, the fuse wire melts and breaks the circuit.

gas, page 6.
A gas is a state of matter. In a gas, the tiny particles of matter are far apart from one another.

generator, page 44.
A generator is a device that makes electricity by electromagnetic induction. Water or steam turbines are used to run generators.

gravity, page 102.
Gravity is a force that attracts, or pulls on, matter. On Earth, gravity attracts all matter to the ground.

heat energy, page 36.
Heat energy is energy passed as heat from one object to another.

inclined plane, page 116.
An inclined plane is a flat surface that slopes, such as a ramp.

inert gas, page 14.
An inert gas is a gas that is slow to combine with other elements. Helium is an inert gas.

input device, page 126.
An input device is used to enter information into a computer. A keyboard is a common input device.

insulator, page 76.
An insulator is a kind of matter that electrons cannot move through easily. Rubber is a good insulator.

iris, page 70.
The iris is the colored part of the eye. The iris changes the size of the pupil to let in the right amount of light.

larynx, page 62.
The larynx, or voice box, is the top part of the windpipe. It holds the vocal cords that produce speech.

laser, page 128.
A laser is a machine that makes light that is much stronger than natural light. Laser light has waves of only one wavelength, all traveling in the same direction.

lenses, page 68.
Lenses are pieces of glass or other materials that can bend light.

lever, page 116.
A lever is a rod that can turn on a point, called a fulcrum. If you push down on the end of one kind of lever, the other end moves up.

liquid, page 6.
A liquid is a state of matter. In a liquid, the tiny particles of matter are farther apart than in a solid. A liquid takes the shape of its container.

magnet, page 84.
A magnet is a metal that can attract and repel other pieces of metal.

magnetic field, page 84.
A magnetic field is an attracting area around a magnet.

magnetism, page 84.
Magnetism is a pulling force that certain metals have.

mass, page 4.
Mass is a measure of how much matter an object has. The mass of an object never changes.

matter, page 4.
Matter is anything that takes up space and has mass. The whole world is made of matter.

mechanical energy, page 36.
Whenever anything moves, it is using mechanical energy.

metal, page 12.
A metal is an element that conducts heat and electricity. Many metals are shiny and are easy to shape. Most elements are metals.

metalloid, page 14.
A metalloid is an element that is shiny like a metal but does not conduct heat and electricity well. Silicon is a metalloid.

microchip, page 90.
A microchip is a small piece of silicon that holds many transistors.

mixture, page 22.
A mixture is a combination of elements and compounds in which no new substances are formed.

molecule, page 20.
A molecule is a group of atoms. Most matter can be broken down into molecules.

motion, page 96.
Motion means moving. An object is in motion only in relation to other objects.

neutron, page 8.
A neutron is a particle in the nucleus of an atom. It has no electric charge.

nonmetal, page 14.
A nonmetal is an element that is not like a metal. Nonmetals can be solids, liquids, or gases. Carbon, oxygen, and nitrogen are nonmetals.

nuclear energy, page 48.
Nuclear energy is the energy given off when the nuclei of atoms split.

nuclear reactor, page 48.
A nuclear reactor is a place where nuclear energy is produced.

nucleus, page 8.
The nucleus is the center of an atom. Protons and neutrons are in the nucleus.

optic nerve, page 70.
The optic nerve in the eye sends messages from the retina to the brain. The brain sees the messages as pictures.

output device, page 126.
An output device displays the information that is in a computer. Most computers have a screen as an output device.

percussion instrument, page 58.
A percussion instrument makes sounds by being struck. A drum is a percussion instrument.

periodic table, page 16.
The periodic table is a scientific chart that lists all 109 elements. The elements are arranged in rows according to their atomic numbers.

photon, page 64.
A photon is a tiny particle of light that has no mass. Photons travel in waves.

physical change, page 24.
A physical change is any change in matter that does not change the matter's molecules. When matter changes states, a physical change takes place.

pitch, page 56.
The pitch of a sound is the quality of being high or low. A sound's pitch is the same as the frequency of its sound waves.

plasma, page 6.
Plasma is a state of matter that is not common on Earth. The sun, most of the stars, and lightning are plasma.

pole, page 84.
A pole is the end of a magnet. All magnets have a north pole and a south pole.

prism, page 67.
A prism is a piece of glass shaped like a triangle. A prism separates light into its different colors.

program, page 126.
A program is a set of instructions for a computer.

proton, page 8.
A proton is a particle in the nucleus of an atom. It has a positive electric charge.

pulley, page 116.
A pulley is a wheel with a rope around it. Pulleys can be used to lift objects.

pupil, page 70.
The pupil is a hole in the middle of the eye. Light enters the eye through the pupil. The size of the pupil is changed by the iris to let in the right amount of light.

radiation, page 40.
Radiation is one way of passing heat energy. Radiation moves in waves. Heat comes from the sun in radiation waves.

rays, page 64.
Light travels in straight lines called rays.

reflection, page 64.
Reflection takes place when light rays hit a smooth surface and bounce back.

refraction, page 64.
Refraction takes place when light rays are bent by things in their path.

retina, page 70.
The retina is the lining at the back of the eye. It is attached to the optic nerve.

robot, page 130.
A robot is a machine that can do tasks by itself. Most robots have computers inside them.

rotate, page 66.
To rotate means to spin around. Earth rotates.

salt, page 30.
A salt is a compound that is formed when an acid and an alkali neutralize each other.

satellite, pages 106, 132.
A satellite is an object that orbits, or moves around, Earth. The moon is a natural satellite.

screw, page 116.
A screw is an inclined plane wrapped around a rod. Screws hold things together well.

semiconductor, page 90.
A semiconductor is a kind of matter that is not a very good conductor or insulator. It can control an electric current in an electronic device.

short circuit, page 78.
In a short circuit, electrical wires that should be separate touch each other. Then electrons can move from wire to wire, taking a shortcut through the circuit. A short circuit can start a fire.

silicon, page 90.
Silicon is an element that is used as a semiconductor.

simple machine, page 116.
A simple machine is a device that makes work easier. All machines are based on the six simple machines: the lever, inclined plane, wedge, screw, pulley, and wheel and axle.

solar energy, page 38.
Solar energy is energy from the sun. On Earth, solar energy is changed to other kinds of energy.

solid, page 6.
A solid is a state of matter. In a solid, the tiny particles of matter are held very closely together. A solid holds its shape.

solution, page 22.
A solution is a mixture in which one substance is dissolved in another. Most solutions are liquids, but some are solids.

spectrum, page 67.
The spectrum is all the colors of light. The spectrum can be seen through the use of a prism.

speed, page 98.
Speed is the distance something moves in a certain time.

state, page 6.
A state is a form of matter. Matter can exist in four states: solid, liquid, gas, and plasma.

static electricity, page 76.
Static electricity is the movement of electrically charged particles in many directions.

steam, page 46.
When water boils, it turns into a gas called steam. Steam can push on objects and move them.

steam energy, page 46.
Steam energy is the energy that comes from the push of steam.

steam turbine, page 46.
A steam turbine is a kind of wheel with blades. Steam turbines can turn a ship's propellers. They can also be used to make electricity.

stringed instrument, page 58.
A stringed instrument makes sounds by vibrating strings. A guitar is a stringed instrument.

superconductor, page 134.
A superconductor is a material that does not resist the flow of electricity.

technology, page 132.
Technology is the use of science to develop new machines.

terminal, page 82.
A terminal is a post of a dry cell. One terminal is negative, and the other is positive. When a wire is put between the two terminals, a circuit is made.

transistor, page 90.
A transistor is a tiny device used to change current electricity into signals.

trough, page 54.
The trough is the lowest part of a wave.

velocity, page 98.
Velocity is speed in a certain direction.

vocal cords, page 62.
The vocal cords are small bands of tissue on either side of the voice box, or larynx. Vibrations of the vocal cords are the sounds that make up speech.

volts, page 78.
The amount of push a source of electricity gives the electricity is measured in volts. The number of volts tells how easily the current can move through a circuit.

water energy, page 44.
Water energy is energy that comes from the push of water. Water energy can turn waterwheels or turbines.

water turbine, page 44.
A water turbine is a device that turns water energy into mechanical energy. This energy can be used to run a generator that makes electricity.

wavelength, page 54.
Wavelength is the distance between the crests of two waves.

wedge, page 116.
A wedge is two inclined planes that come together in a point.

wheel and axle, page 116.
A wheel and axle is a kind of lever that continues to turn around its fulcrum.

wind energy, page 42.
Wind energy is the energy of moving air. Wind energy can power sailboats and turn windmills.

wind instrument, page 58.
A wind instrument makes sounds by a vibrating column of air inside the instrument. A saxophone is a wind instrument.

windpipe, page 62.
The windpipe is a tube in the throat. Air moving up through the windpipe makes the vocal cords vibrate. Then sounds are made.

work, page 110.
Work is the use of force to move an object.

ACKNOWLEDGEMENTS

Staff Credits

Executive Editor: Elizabeth Strauss

Project Editor: Susan Miller

Design Coordinator: Cynthia Ellis

Product Development

Contemporary **cpi** Perspectives, Inc.

Illustrations

Alex Bloch—**98, 100, 102, 104, 110, 112, 114, 116, 117, 118, 120**

Erika Kors—**4, 8, 12, 20, 22, 24, 28, 30, 32, 40, 56, 58, 60, 62, 82, 84, 96, 97, 128, 132**

Tek-Nek, Inc.—**6, 16, 54**

Stephen Turner—**66**

All Other Illustrations

Ben Smith and Jessie Flores

Photographs

Cover   Harald Sund/The Image Bank

American Airlines—**122**

Calderon—**14L**

Caterpillar Inc.—**86**

Chevrolet—**36R**

Christiana Dittmann/Rainbow—**10T**

David Doody/Tom Stack—**50R**

Fermilab—**134**

T.J. Florian/Rainbow—**14R**

Ford Motor Company—**120L**

General Motors Corp.—**130**

Jeff Greenberg—**64B**

Grant Heilman—**48, 50L**

Michal Heron—**26L**

Dan McCox/Rainbow—**10B**

Viki Miller/in Stock—**26R**

Linda S. Mueller—**88**

National Weather Service—**74**

NC Industrial—**90**

NOAA—**106**

Jeanne Payne—**80**

Carl Purcell/Words and Pictures—**10M**

Anthony V. Ragusin—**42L**

Manuel Rodriguez—**67T**

Tatiana Sayig—**126**

Kevin Schafer—**42R**

Victoria Beller Smith—**92**

U.S. Department of the Interior—**44B**

USUBA—**36L**